ABU SIMBEL

ASWAN AND THE NUBIAN TEMPLES

G000068187

BONECHI

Concept and Project: *Casa Editrice Bonechi*
Series Editor: *Giovanna Magi*
Graphic design: *Manuela Ranfagni*
Picture Research: *Giovanna Magi*
Cover: *Manuela Ranfagni*
Layout: *Patrizia Fabbri*
Texts: *Giovanna Magi, Patrizia Fabbri*
Editing: *Patrizia Fabbri*
Drawing on pages 60-61: *Stefano Benini*

© Copyright by Casa Editrice Bonechi - Florence - Italy
E-mail: bonechi@bonechi.it

Printed in Italy by *Centro Stampa Editoriale Bonechi*.

The photographs are the property of the *Casa Editrice Bonechi* Archives.

Other contributors:
Archivi Alinari, Florence: page 28.
Art Archive/Gianni Dagli Orti: pages 30 left and bottom, 52 centre, 53 top, 56 bottom, 62.
Getty Images by Laura Ronchi: pages 18, 76 bottom, 77.
Alain Guilleux: page 126.
Andrea Jemolo: page 66 top.
Marie Josephine Kassasseya: pages 68-69.
Giacomo Lovera: pages 10 bottom left, 42-49, 84/85, 97.
Roger-Viollet/Archivi Alinari, Florence: pages 82/83.
Sie-Simephoto: pages 58, 59 bottom, 67 top, 70 bottom, 127 bottom.
Altitude/TIPS Images: page 19 bottom.
Mario Tosi: pages 7, 9 bottom, 14/15, 19 top, 100-125, 127 top and centre, 128.
© *UNESCO/Nenadovic*: pages 22, 26, 27.

The publisher apologizes for any errors or omissions concerning credits and will be pleased to acknowledge them in future editions.

ISBN 978-88-476-1913-5

www.bonechi.com

* * *

CONTENTS

The Temples
of Lower Nubia

Abu Simbel
The Great Temple

Abu Simbel
The Small Temple

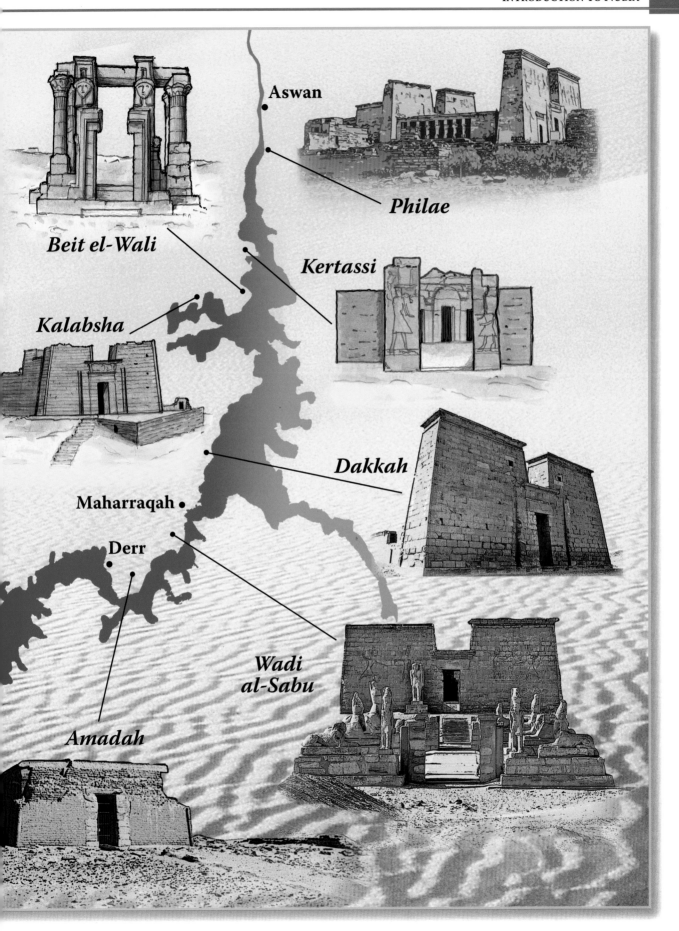

Beit el-Wali

Aswan

Philae

Kertassi

Kalabsha

Dakkah

Maharraqah

Derr

Wadi
al-Sabu

Amadah

GOING UP THE NILE
Lower Nubia between history and legend

Flying over Lower Nubia, the legendary kingdom of the "black pharaohs," today's traveller heading towards Abu Simbel will inevitably be fascinated by the panorama that unfolds beneath his eyes. It is as surreal as it is rich in contrasts with its infinite sky, an enormous expanse of water, practically a "little blue sea", and all around an endless sandy desert with outcroppings of black volcanic rock that wind has sculpted through the ages. The huge lake (approximately 500 km long – of which 150 are in Sudanese territory – and 5 to 10 km wide) straddling the border between Egypt and the Sudan is a recent arrival in the area, and it has markedly changed the physiognomies of these places.

The Egyptians call it "Nasser" while for the Sudanese it is "Nuba", and it is the most amazing result or by-product of the construction of the High Aswan Dam (*Saad el-Aali*). The dam project had another epoch-making consequence: it forced the world to mobilize in order to save an extraordinary cultural and historical heritage. And so it happened that in 1963 the majestic temples of Lower Nubia, destined to be submerged by the lake were, to a large extent dismantled or cut, moved to stable safe land and rebuilt. Thus the new dam thrust this vast area back into the limelight: a region traversed by the Nile, and which in past millennia had played a very long and important role.

Typical images of Nubia: white feluccas gliding along the Nile and the endless deserts studded with volcanic rock formations.

Indeed, the colonization of Lower Nubia can be traced back to the Egyptians and specifically the Old Kingdom, and the 4th Dynasty (around 2600 B.C.) when repeated expeditions pushed as far as the Second Cataract of the Nile. The actual conquest, however, can be dated in the era of the Middle Kingdom and specifically the 12th dynasty (1955-1790 B.C.), under whose sovereigns the first monuments and mainly fortresses were built in Lower Nubia. It was Sesostris III who established the southern boundary of Egypt at Semna during the eighth year of his reign and built two fortresses, one at Semna West and the other at Kumma (Semna East).

Later, during the New Kingdom, at the time of the 18th dynasty (around 1552-1306 B.C.), some rulers such as the great Tuthmosis III, his son Amenhotep II and grandson Tuthmosis IV built many majestic temples, just to mention a few, Kalabsha, Amadah and the pillared vestibule opposite the sanctuary of Amada, which no longer exists. Perhaps the pharaohs' reasons for building these sanctuaries was to present tangible evidence of their power and thus obtain

even the religious support of the local populations. The great pharaoh, Ramses II, of the 19th dynasty also wanted to pursue colonization and on a grand scale. He decided to build monuments in the region between the First and Second Cataracts of the Nile, that is Aswan. And so, in a narrow strip of Nubian territory that runs for around 300 km along the banks of the Nile he built, in addition to the temples of Abu Simbel, five entirely rock-cut or part masonry sanctuaries: Beit el-Wali, Gerf Hussein, Wadi es-Sebua, Derr, Aksha or Serra West. The Nubian temples built by Ramses were probably created as stopping places for Amon-Ra, the god who cast off from the Elephantine Island, sailed along the river to Aniba and Abu Simbel and then returned to Egypt. However, the sanctuaries had other important purposes as well which were linked to specific religious reasons. The three main gods of the Egyptian pantheon, Amon, Ra and Ptah, present in all Nubian temples had to create an unique image of divinity and the effigy of the sovereign stood in the cellae of these sanctuaries along with the three gods to signify that the pharaoh, too,

The Great Temple and Small Temple of Abu Simbel, brilliantly reconstructed beyond the range of Lake Nasser dominate the landscape in splendid majesty.

was an aspect of the divine essence. And since Ramses II in particular wanted to be taken as the incarnation of the god Ra, deified like the sun, he was particularly partial to Nubia which the Egyptians considered the land of gold and of the sun because it was the place closest to where the sun rose and hence the privileged place for the worship of Ra and the king who was his incarnation.

Nubia, with its strategic position for trade with Africa, the great market for exotic goods, gold, minerals, and rare wood had, enjoyed several periods of governmental auto-nomy. Indeed, at one point a Nubian dynasty held the throne of Egypt, it was the 25th dynasty that reigned between 713 and 664 B.C. Defeated first by the Assyrians and then by the pharaoh Psammetichus II, of the 26th dynasty, the Nubians returned to their own lands known as the "Kingdom of Kush", with its capital first at Napata and then at Meroe, generating an original culture that was to flourish for more than another thousand years before it succumbed to the Ethiopian kingdom of Axum and the encroaching desert.

Exploring *NUBIA*

The spell of Nubia, a desert land rich in mineral resources, scoured in ancient times by Nero's centurions and Arabian explorers once again began to lure scholars and adventurers with its seductive and mysterious exoticism in the second half of the nineteenth century. They were drawn by prospect of finding precious treasures and extraordinary artefacts and many came to the legendry and majestic Nubian tombs. Nubia had long been filled with tales of inestimable riches that were supposedly hidden in the pyramids scattered throughout the urban fabric of the ancient capital of Meroe as well as in the rock-carved tombs and the ruins of the temples that dotted the immense desert.

However, this reawakening of interest must be historically tied to Napoleon's famous military expedition to Egypt which between 1798 and 1800 saw a large group of scientists alongside of the French troops, charged with conducting historical, archaeological, geographic and linguistic studies. This was the first philological approach to the vestiges of what had been an ancient and splendid civilization. Even in the following years, scholars followed in each others' footsteps across the sands of the Egyptian deserts, from Bernardino Drovetti to Count De Forbin. But, it was to be another expedition, Franco-Tuscan this time, that opened the doors of Nubia to the world. Financed by the grand duke Leopoldo II of Tuscany and king Charles X of France this venture, begun in July 1828 and concluded in December 1829, led scholars of the calibre of Jean-François Champollion and Ippolito Rosellini, who on the basis of this experience wrote an important and most interesting book *Monument of Egypt and Nubia*, published between 1832 and 1844, to go up the Nile as far as the Second Cataract and discover treasures the likes of which only a few Europeans had an opportunity to admire up to then.

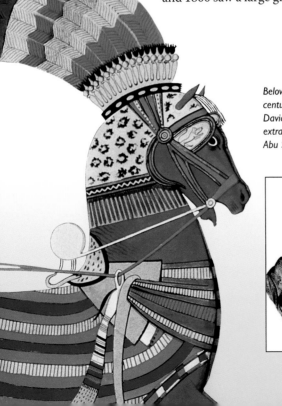

Below, portraits of some of the men who explored Egypt and Nubia in the nineteenth century: from the left, Ippolito Rossellini, Giovanni Battista Belzoni and the English artist, David Roberts who, during the eleven months he spent here (1838-1839), created extraordinary images (opposite page, two of his famous drawings: top, the temples of Abu Simbel still buried in the sand and below, the temple of Kalabsha).

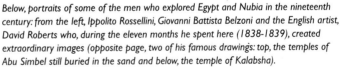

In fact, in 1738 probably just sailing a boat and without going ashore, the Dane Frederick Norden, an officer of king Christian VI, got this far, but he probably never went beyond Derr, then capital of Lower Nubia. To go beyond it was the Swiss explorer Johann Ludwig Burchardt, who in 1813 became enchanted with Abu Simbel and recommended it as a destination for William Bankes of England.

Bernardino Drovetti, former Consul General of France reached Abu Simbel, with its temples still buried in the sand, in 1826. In the autumn of that same year he was followed by the Paduan Giovanni Battista Belzoni. In 1817 Belzoni went as far as the Second Cataract of the Nile, flanked by English officers. Then he concentrated all his efforts on freeing the ruins of the temples of Abu Simbel from the sands, while the many later expeditions were engaged mainly in reaching and going beyond the Second Cataract.

So, after the Franco-Tuscan expedition, with its concrete objective of finding artefacts and treasures, in 1834 an Italian physician, Giuseppe Ferlini arrived in Nubia. He was with Egyptian troops as medical officer of the Egyptian army stationed in the Sudan. It is to him that we are indebted for the discovery of many antiquities (155 objects or sets of objects including 88 in gold, 8 in silver, some bronzes and various stones), that were brought to Italy and after

Another nineteenth century drawing by David Roberts: a front view of the Great Temple of Abu Simbel with the four colossi portraying the seated pharaoh Ramses II and the immense, falcon-headed statue of Ra-Harakhti, still half-buried by the desert sands.

GIOVANNI BATTISTA BELZONI

(Padua 1778-Gwato, West Africa, 1823) – Italian explorer and archaeologist. After studying engineering in Rome, Belzoni moved to England. In 1815, he was commissioned by the British Museum to travel to Egypt to collect archaeological remains. Thus not only did he bring the enormous bust of Ramses II from Thebes, but also opened the entrance to the great temple of Abu Simbel and directed the excavations at Karnak. In 1817 he entered the Valley of the Kings where he discovered the tomb of Seti I. In 1818 he had the privilege of being the first (or almost...) to enter Khafre's pyramid.

A typical Nubian landscape on the shores of Lake Nasser.

his death subjected to many vicissitudes, that led to their being scattered if not entirely lost.

By that time expeditions to Egypt and Nubia had lost part of their adventurous and romantic character and were becoming increasingly scientific, supported by appropriate equipment and a proper philological and archaeological approach. This was true for Robert Hay's journey (1831), which marked the birth of English Egyptology and would also hold true for the much more famous journey of the Prussian Karl Richard Lepsius, who for

two years, between 1842 and 1843, with an efficient team worked among the monuments of Nubia, transcribing inscriptions, making surveys, and studying temples and tombs in great detail.

That period also marked the beginning of what can properly be called tours undertaken by the wealthy as well as by enthusiastic artists such as David Roberts and enterprising journalists who made a substantial contribution to arousing increasing interest in Egyptology and the great monuments of this ancient civilization throughout

the world. In this sense, the work of Gaston Maspero, Director General of the Department of Antiquities of Egypt, was fundamental. He was greatly interested in Nubia and its enormous treasures that were too often abandoned to undeserved oblivion. At the turn of the nineteenth-twentieth century he drew many scholars – mainly from England, France and Germany to these desert lands. They worked for long periods and conducted countless studies of the Nubian ruins. And he was the first to raise the issue of dangers to the Nubian temples caused by the rising of the height of the first dam built at Aswan. It was most useful for supplying water, but had already caused problems towards the south by raising the level of the Nile. Therefore, Maspero was the first to fight for saving the great temples anticipating what would become a truly global mobilization by more than half a century.

Two more drawings by the talented hand of David Roberts showing the Island of Philae (right) and a detail of Trajan's Pavilion (above) that stands on the southern tip of the island.

Today, archaeological researches in Nubia still hold interesting surprises, and not just in terms of discoveries and finds: archaeologists are gradually defining and clarifying the profile of a civilization that played a leading role on the stage of the African continent and that had maintained fruitful relationships with contemporary cultures. By increasing our knowledge of Nubia, we have been able to note a marked cultural similarity between the peoples of Central Africa and those of the Mediterranean dominated by the Roman Empire. Indeed, Nubia can no longer be considered a "suburb" of the pharaohs' Egypt, but rather an autonomous entity capable of offering the world not only precious minerals and rare woods, but also – and above all – the heritage of an original culture enriched by continued and varied relationships with the leading civilizations of the ancient world.

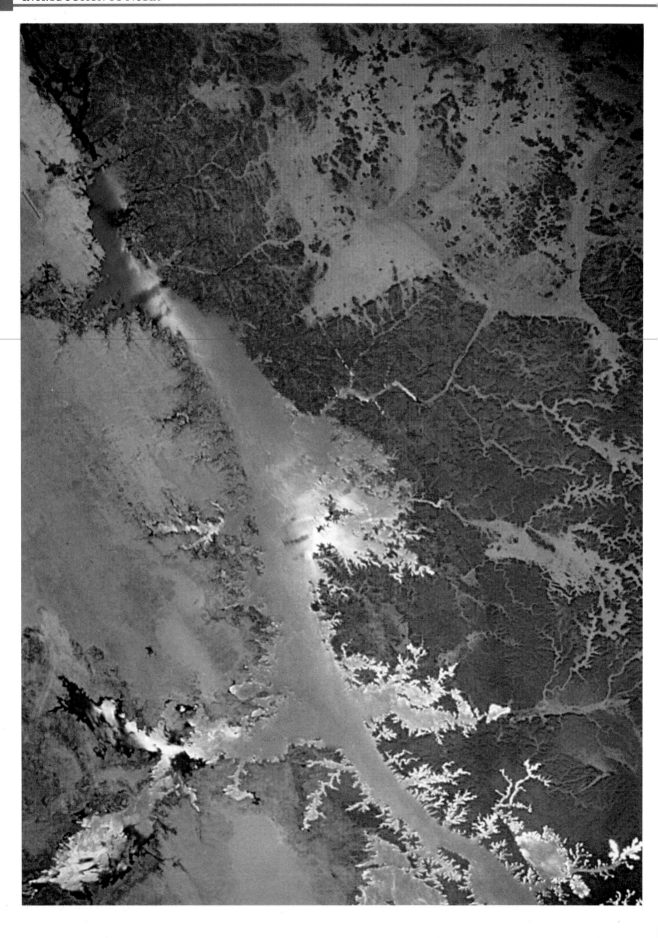

THE TERRITORY
A bit of geography

Geographically speaking, Nubia is a vast region between Aswan on the north and the confluence of the White and Blue Niles in Sudan to the south. It is a long strip of desert entirely traversed by the Nile which extends for nearly 1000 km as the crow flies. It is conventionally divided into Lower Nubia (the northernmost section that is part of Egypt) and Upper Nubia (the southern part that belongs to the Sudan). Lower Nubia, between the First and Second Cataracts of the Nile was called *Uauat* by the Egyptians, Upper Nubia, the Egyptian's *Kush* opens to the south of the Second Cataract. In fact, one of the region's peculiarities is the course of the river itself which is more placid here than usual, partly because of a higher gradient of the riverbed which with two loops and a series of rapids and the succession of six Cataracts, drops from an altitude of 350 metres above sea level to 90. All around, the endless desolate stretch of Nubian desert is broken by the long and very jagged blue contours of Lake Nasser. This artificial lake was generated by the Aswan Dam. In addition to countless sites it also submerged nearly two thirds of the ancient arable lands, but on the other hand, it offers an immense water source that can be also used for irrigation. It is immense, important and has led to a radical change in the lives of the Nubian people.

The creation of Lake Nasser has given Nubia a very peculiar shape that is easily recognizable even from satellite images.

ABU SIMBEL
History

*S*ome three hundred kilometres from Aswan, in the region of Nubia, lying almost on the border with Sudan, is a strikingly beautiful and majestic monument built by the most powerful pharaoh in the history of Egypt: the temple of Abu Simbel, in theory dedicated to the deities Amon-Ra, Ra-Harakhti and Ptah, but actually erected for the eternal glorification of Ramses II himself.

Abu Simbel is not just one of the most beautiful temples in Egypt – it is certainly the most unusual and imposing – but is also symbolic of the vast enterprise undertaken to save the 14 temples of Nubia that were threatened by the rising waters of Lake Nasser. The fact that the temple would be submerged by the lake was a danger that alarmed the entire world.

And while Abu Simbel was the most beautiful and impressive of the Nubian temples, it was also the most difficult to save given the material from which it was made, its location and the design of its structure. Despite the problems, however, sheer determination and the wonders of technology combined to achieve one of the most incredible feats of dismantelling and reconstruction ever undertaken by archaeologists, thus saving the temple and perpetuating its memory throughout the centuries.

Left and below, two images showing the temples of Abu Simbel today, reconstructed in a safe location beyond the reach of the water.

The face of Ramses II at Abu Simbel is characterized by a most serene expression. At the time of the discovery Burckhardt described it in the following words: "The face on the head emerging from the sand is young and very expressive and closer to Greek beauty than to any other ancient Egyptian statue I have ever seen."

The rescue of the temples of Abu Simbel

© UNESCO/Nenadovic

For many centuries the two rock-cut temples of Abu-Simbel on the banks of the Nile were seen not only as a memorial to the power and deification of Ramses II, but as the achievement of an architectural and technical challenge – a challenge that two thousand years later faced engineers and technicians from around the world again. The danger that the temples would be submerged by the waters of Lake Nasser drew global attention and the temple became symbolic of the campaign to save all the monuments of Nubia. Between 10 and 12 June 1963 the Egyptian government gave its final approval to a project that involved complete removal of the entire mass of rock by cutting the temple into blocks and subsequently rebuilding it in a higher location. The rescue operation was immensely complex and involved the organization of thousands of workmen and engineers. The task was also a furious race against time. Work began in April 1964 but already by the end of the summer the waters of the artificial lake had risen more rapidly than expected. Just some figures: 1,036 blocks with an average weight of 30 tons each were moved, while a further 1,112 were cut from the rock around the

Images that are history: the immense undertaking of dismantling the temples of Abu Simbel was made possible thanks international cooperation.

© UNESCO/Nenadovic

On these pages, historic photos documenting the almost superhuman task of dismantling the temples of Abu Simbel. This was the only way to save a great heritage for mankind.

temples and 33 tons of resin were used to consolidate the rock structure - it was the most incredible project of dismantelling and reconstruction that archaeologists had ever attempted. The two temples were rebuilt on ground 90 metres higher, exactly as before. It was realised however, that straightforward reconstruction was not possible as the weight of the artificial mountain covering the monument would have crushed it. Two enormous domes of reinforced concrete were therefore built to bear the pressure from the mountain above and so protect the temples like an enormous bell. The backfill was used to cover the concrete domes and the sand itself would rapidly fill in the cracks. Work finished on 22 September 1968 – barely in time as the waters were already slowly flowing into the enormous, desolately empty caverns left below. The vast rock complex above was completed and, as punctually as ever, in 1969 the "miracle of the sun" occurred just as before. Once again, the rays of the sun illuminated the gods within the sanctuary as they had done for three thousand years. Despite everything, Ramses II and his architectural masterpiece continue to survive.

© UNESCO/Nenadovic

In order to be able to reconstruct the temples of Abu Simbel on the new sites, they had to be cut into pieces and dismantled with utmost care and scientific precision.

The writer, André Malraux (1901-1976) was French Minister of Culture in 1958 and 1959. Below are some excerpts from his speech to UNESCO at the opening of the global campaign to save the temples of Nubia.

For the first time, on 8 March 1960, precisely at a time when many of them are involved in a secret or declared war, all nations are called upon to save the works of a civilization that belongs to none of them. [...] These magnificent temples were, above all, witnesses, now the only ones that we have inherited from the Ancient Orient: and what witnesses they are, these catalaptic masterpieces that for three thousand years seemed to be united in the same eternal sleep. [...]

The survival of Egypt lies with her art, not with illustrious names or strings of victories. [...] Despite Kadesh, one of the decisive battles in history, despite the cartouches, shattered and newly engraved by order of the intrepid pharaoh eager to impose his

descendancy on the gods, Senusret is less known to us today than poor Akhenaton. And our artists are obsessed by the face of queen Nefertiti, just as Cleopatra tormented our poets. But Cleopatra was a queen that has no face, and Nefertiti is a face that has no queen. [...]

For the first time humanity has discovered a universal language of art. [...]

Look, old river whose tides enabled astrologers to establish the most ancient date in history, the men who will move these colossi far from your fertile yet devastating waters are arriving from all over the world. Night falls, and once again you reflect the constellations beneath which Isis performed funerary rituals, the star that Ramses beheld. But even the most humble of the workmen that will save the images of Isis and Ramses will tell you what you have always known but will hear for the first time, "There is only one action over which indifferent stars and unchanging rivers have no sway: it is the action of a man who snatches something from death."

Burckhardt and Belzoni: the discovery

*I*t is a strange fact that Abu Simbel, now considered one of the most famous monuments of Egypt, was almost totally unknown even as late as the 19th century. Ybsambul had become little more than a legend. The story of the site begins on 22 March 1813 when Johann Ludwig Burckhardt, a Swiss historian, known to the Arabs as Ibrahim ibn Abdallah, landed on this bank of the Nile accompanied by the local guide Saad to visit the temple of Nefertari, convinced that the temple dedicated to the beautiful and adored wife of the pharaoh was the only antiquity of Abu Simbel. He was just about to climb back up the sandy slope "... when by a lucky chance I took a few steps further to the south and my eyes fell on what is still visible of four colossal statues, cut from the rock." The strong wind had blown the sand dozens of metres down the gorge, heaping it ever higher against the enormous stone giants and leaving only part of the heads exposed. The blanket of sand left them barely visible and it was impossible for Burckhardt to tell if the statues were standing or sitting. Abu Simbel, the mythical Ybsambul, had, however, been rediscovered. Just four years later, on 1 August 1817, another adventurer, Giovanni Battista Belzoni, the most daring of them all, managed to remove the sand from the upper part of a doorway and discover the entrance. After eleven centuries a European was to break into the architectural masterpiece and personal achievement of Ramses the Great. Following Belzoni, many travellers faced the discomfort and uncertainties of crossing the Nubian desert to arrive at Abu Simbel; all were impressed by the magnificence of the monument and all were moved by the sudden appearance of the gigantic, imposing figures that seemed to emerge from the sand for some fantastic, supernatural event. Scholars too, arrived: the Italians Ippolito Rosellini and Salvatore Cherubini, the French artist, Nestor L'Hôte, François Champollion who wrote that this temple alone made the journey into Nubia worthwhile, the German archaeologist Heinrich Schliemann who had discovered entire cities such as Troy, Mycenae and Tiryns and described the site as "the most powerful work of art in the world". Once the sand had been entirely removed from the façade of the temple, visitors could enter more easily, without fear of finding the entrance suddenly blocked again. At last it was possible to fully appreciate the beauty and complex design of the rock-cut temple of Abu Simbel.

Left, in this late nineteenth century photo we can see that tourists were still allowed to climb onto the pharaoh's head. Above, a period portrait of Johann Ludwig Burckhardt.

THE CONQUEST OF THE GREAT TEMPLE

In his diary, Giovanni Battista Belzoni described the moment of entering the Great Temple of Abu Simbel: "The sand, heaped up against the rock that dominates the temple by the wind coming from the north, had gradually encroached across the façade and buried the entrance by three quarters. Thus the first time that I approached the temple I lost hope of freeing the entrance as it seemed quite impossible to reach the doorway. ... The sand was slipping across from one side to the other of the façade and consequently it was pointless to try to open a straight access towards the entrance; it was thus necessary to excavate in the opposite direction so that the sand fell beyond the façade. ... The morning of the first of August we went to the temple very early, excited by the idea of finally entering the underground chambers that we had uncovered. ... We stepped into the passage we had opened and had the pleasure of being the first to descend into the largest and most beautiful underground chamber in Nubia, and to examine a monument comparable to the most beautiful in all of Egypt.

... We were at first astonished by the immensity of the place; we found magnificent antiquities, paintings, sculptures and massive statues."

Ramses II: the pharaoh and Nefertari

Going by an inscription in the Nubian temple of Wadi es-Sebua, Ramses had fifty sons and fifty-five daughters. Scholars, however, tend to disagree. Champollion and Lepsius give him 160 children, James Breasted calculated nearly 200, and Faruk Gomaa fewer than 100. In any event Ramses II was a very prolific sovereign, even later in life: an *ostracon* conserved in the Louvre reads "a son was born to His Majesty in the 53rd year" when he must have been sixty-five years old.

But, even if scholars disagree as to the number of children, there is no dispute regarding the relationship between the

pharaoh and Nefertari, the Great Royal Wife. Ramses had eight wives, but the most important, and the most beloved was, without a doubt, the first, Nefertari, who was wed while still co-regent, Nefertari-Meri-en-Mut ("beloved of Mut"), the one for whom the pharaoh built the temple "of fine, white solid stone" at Abu Simbel, the one who would be portrayed in statues as tall as those of her husband beside her.

Nefertari, "great of love, beautiful of face, pretty with two feathers, sweet of love, lady of the Two Lands", perhaps descended from the family of Ay. As the main consort of Ramses she was always at his side on official occasions and during religious ceremonies. And it was she who gave him his first son Amon-her-Kopechef.

Nefertari died some time around the thirtieth year of the reign. The most beautiful tomb in the Valley of the Queens was built for her: it recalls the elegant beauty of the queen on the walls and on the pillars. Here the queen offers of wine to Hathor, extending the bowl to the goddess with infinite grace, or she imperiously holds the *sekhem* sceptre before Osiris and Atum, or, with artful makeup and wrapped in a long white tunic she plays the destiny of her soul in the next world at *senet*.

Left: some portrayals of Ramses II, the granite statue conserved In the Egyptian Museum, Cairo, In the colossus on the façade of Abu Simbel and In a black granite bust as a young man with a round wig surmounted by the uraeus and a wide necklace on his finely pleated garment.
Right: the elegant beauty of Nefertari, as she appears on a wall of her tomb In the Valley of the Queens: like all the women of Ancient Egypt, Nefertari had heavily made up eyes.

The Great Temple

*T*he temple of Abu Simbel is an exact transferral of the architectural form of an Egyptian inner sanctuary temple cut deep inside the rock.

Sculpted into the mountain, the *façade* is 38 metres long and 31 high. This is framed by a convex 'torus' moulding, and is surmounted by a cornice with uraei (the sacred asp) above which is carved a row of 22 seated baboons, each two and a half metres high. Below the torus moulding is a cornice engraved with dedicatory hieroglyphics, and in a niche below this in the middle of the façade is a large high-relief statue representing Ra-Harakhti with a falcon's head, flanked by two low-relief figures of Ramses II. Four colossal statues of Ramses II seated form the supporting columns of the façade. Even on this monumental scale they reproduce the true features of the monarch. They are 20 metres high and measure more than 4 from ear to ear, while the lips, measuring over a metre, express a soft, gentle smile. The pharaoh is represented with his hands resting in his lap, wearing the double crown and a headdress with deep folds on either side of his face. The second statue on the left is broken and part of the head and body lie on the ground. Beside and between the legs of each colossus are other statues representing members of the royal family including a daughter (who was also his wife) Bent-Anat, his mother Tuya, his wife Nefertari, his son Amon-her-Kopechef, and another daughter and wife, Merytamun. On the base and along the sides of the seats are figures of African and Asian prisoners. A "multitude of workers imprisoned by his sword" worked on the monumental façade under the orders of Pyay, head of all the sculptors, as we read inside the temple. The work of the sculptors was followed by that of the painters for, at the time of Ramses, the temple was most probably richly painted and decorated.

The majesty and size of the Great Temple of Abu Simbel, make it a true masterpiece of rock-carved architecture. It is characterized by a wealth of carved decorations of which outstanding examples are the statues of Horus in front of the base of the colossus.

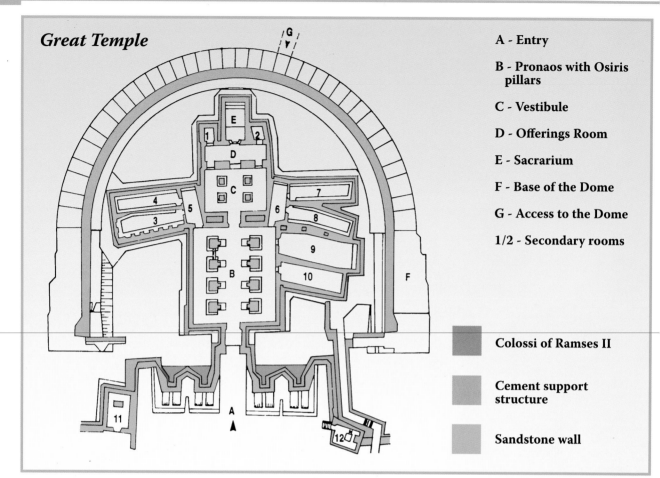

Great Temple

A - Entry

B - Pronaos with Osiris pillars

C - Vestibule

D - Offerings Room

E - Sacrarium

F - Base of the Dome

G - Access to the Dome

1/2 - Secondary rooms

Colossi of Ramses II

Cement support structure

Sandstone wall

Details of the colossi on the façade of the Great Temple of Abu Simbel. The statues on the north side were known as "Ramses beloved of Amon" and "Ramses beloved of Atum," those on the south side were "Ramses sun of the Kings" and "Lord of the two lands."

Below, the row of 22 crouching baboons above the cornice on the façade.

Right: African and Asian prisoners on the base of one of the colossi, that is symbolically standing beneath the pharaoh's feet. Above and below, the statues of members of the royal family between the legs of each colossus.

RA-HARAKHTI

This deity is the supreme personification of the sun and was especially venerated in Heliopoli. The composite form of Ra-Harakhti combines the three various forms of Khepri, Ra and Atum (the rising sun, midday sun and setting sun). The form is anthropomorphic, with a falcon's head, and bears the solar disc. During the fifth dynasty the deity became associated with Amon and became the most important god, Amon-Ra.

View of the pronaos with the Osiris pillars. On the impressive ceiling, crowned vultures with wings spread hold two fans in their talons that protect the cartouche of the pharaoh.

The interior

From the blinding light of day one passes to the interior where the shadowy light emphasises the mysterious and evocative atmosphere. The *pronaos* is a vast rectangular hall 18 metres long and 16.70 wide. This is flanked by eight Osiris pillars ten metres tall arranged in two rows, representing Osiris with the features of Ramses. The colossi on the left wear the white crown of Upper Egypt, those on the right, the "pschent" or double crown. Their arms, crossed over their chests, hold the sceptre and flail. Decorating the roof of the central nave is the great vulture of the goddess Nekhbet, protrectress of Upper Egypt, while the aisles on either side are painted with stars.

*A wall painting shows the pharaoh flanked by gods, including ithyphallic Min,
with two high plumes and raised arm holding the flail.*

"We entered the hall which is fifty seven feet long and fifty two feet wide, supported by a colonnade of square pilasters. Each pilaster is sculpted with a figure; their heads reaching the roof, these caryatids, similar to those of Medinet Habu, are extremely well-made and are little damaged by time. Their pedestals measure five and a half square feet and are engraved with fine hieroglyphs as too are the walls, in a style which is superior to and certainly more lively than normal Egyptian hieroglyphs both in their execution and choice of subject. They describe battles, attacks on fortified castles, triumphs over the Ethiopians, sacrifices etc. ... Some of the columns have been broken by the heat in the enclosed atmosphere, heat that during our visit was still so great that the thermometer would have exceeded one hundred and thirty degrees had the fluid been able to rise that high."

(**Giovanni Battista Belzoni,**
Journeys in Egypt and Nubia.)

The frescoes inside the Great Temple of Abu Simbel always portray the pharaoh flanked by gods. Below left, a detail of the Osiris pillars with the pharaoh wearing the crown of Upper Egypt.

Ippolito Rosellini
and the Franco-Tuscan expedition

Niccolò Ippolito Rosellini, universally acknowledged as the father of Italian Egyptology was born in Pisa on 13 August 1800 and it was there that he died of tuberculosis on 4 June 1843.

After he earned a degree in theology in 1821, he spent three years specializing in Oriental languages in Bologna and ob- tained the chair in Orien- tal Languages and Culture at the University of Pisa.

In 1825, in Florence, he met Jean-François Cham- pollion, who was viewing

Ramses II, seated on field stool with a cushion, discussing the battle plan with his officers learns that the Hittite army is hiding behind the city of Kadesh waiting to attack. In the lower section, a line of soldiers from the pharaoh's personal guard. Not all are Egyptian: we can recognize the Shardana or Sherden, pirates who had been taken prisoner and then impressed into the Egyptian army. They are identified by their round shields and helmets decorated with a disk and two horns. Tradition has it that Island of Sardinia gets Its name from the ancient Shardana.

the Italian collections. That moment marked the beginning of a partnership based on friendship and shared scientific and historical interests. Thanks to the personal, but mainly financial, support of the Grand Duke of Tuscany Leopoldo II, Rosellini was able to make some journeys through Italy and to France with Champollion. It was during a stay in Paris that Rosellini met and married Zenobia, daughter of the composer Luigi Cherubini. It was always thanks to the financial generosity of the grand duke, as well as of the King of France, Charles X that Champollion and Rosellini were able to undertake a joint mission to Egypt. The French scientific expedition was headed by Champollion, the Tuscan literary expedition by Rosellini. The Franco-Tuscan expedition sailed from Toulon on 31 July 1828, it was to have travelled up the Nile Valley as far as Wadi Halfa. Members of the party included painters such as Cherubini, Angelelli, Duchesne, Bertin, Lehoux, draftsmen such as Nestor L'Hôte, the naturalists Giuseppe Raddi and Felice Galastri, archaeologists such as Lenormant, and doctors, such as Alessandro Ricci from Siena.

The scene in this plate (which is n. LXXIX) is on the wall left of the main entrance, after the pronaos, of the Temple of Abu Simbel. Ramses II is shown sacrificing a group of prisoners to Amon-Ra, the different skin colours denote their races: they are Syrian, Libyan and Ethiopian. The pharaoh wears the double crown and elaborate battle armour, while the god wearing the classic tiara with the double feather and extends the khepech sword to the pharaoh. The long inscription behind Ramses includes one of his five names, the "name of Horus" written in a rectangle surmounted by a falcon while the other four names to which he was entitled are inscribed in the scrolls.

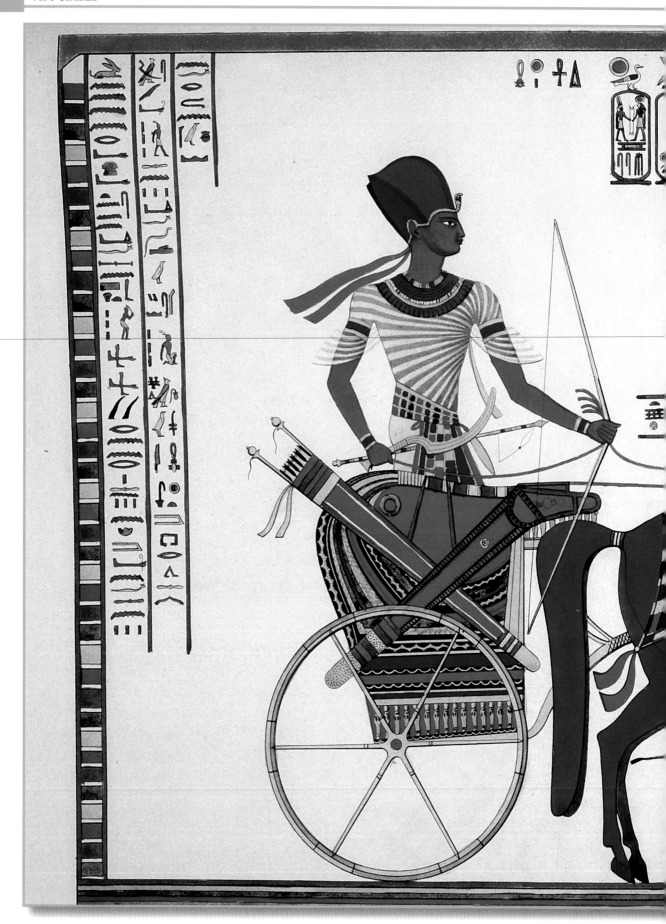

One of the goals of the expedition that lasted from July 1828 to December 1829, was to transfer some items to the Louvre and to Florence. The extraordinary number of objects they found were to comprise the main cores of the Egyptian sections of both museums. The expedition's other objective was to recover as many documents as possible on Egyptian monuments.

Upon their return home Champollion and Rosellini began working on the publication of the expedition's results, but on 4 March 1832 the French Egyptologist, the one who had revealed the secret of the hieroglyphics to the world died at just 42 years of age leaving the bulk of the work to Rosellini. Having become the sole curator of all the documentation the Tuscan dedicated the last years of his life to the task .

Monuments of Egypt and Nubia was published between 1832 and 1836 in eight octavo volumes and two Atlases in folio. The ninth volume and third Atlas were printed posthumously in 1844, edited by two of Rosellini's colleagues, Francesco Bonaini and Flaminio Severi. This monumental publication was divided into three parts "Historical Monuments" (five volumes on Egyptian history), "Civil Monuments" (three volumes on daily life) and "Religious Monuments" (one volume on religion). Midway between a scientific document and work of art (some of the splendid illustrations were hand water-coloured), Rosellini's opus conveys the liveliness, freshness and riches of the Egyptian frescoes with great immediacy. As the authors noted, all the monuments of Egypt and Nubia, from the pyramids to the Second Cataract, were "stripped" so to speak of the historical information carved or written onto the walls and main temples, everything was carefully copied, to have the certainty that nothing important or unusual was overlooked.

Pages 46-47 show plate n. LXXXIV, the decorations on the south wall of the pronaos of the Temple of Abu Simbel. The scene, with the pharaoh standing in a chariot drawn by a finely caparisoned horse, does not- as would seem - portray a battle but rather a triumphal procession celebrating the pharaoh's victory over the Africans.

On the right, plate LXXXV completes the preceding illustration with two groups of Nubian and Ethiopian prisoners dressed in animal skins and chained to each other by the neck.

The divinity of Ramses II was exalted in the iconography inside the Sanctuary of Abu Simbel; he is flanked by the gods Ptah, Amon-Ra and Ra-Harakhti in the group of statues at the back of the niche.

The Sanctuary and the "miracle of the sun"

Sixty-five metres from the entrance, deep in the heart of the mountain, is the sanctuary, the most intimate and secret part of the temple, a small room four metres by seven. Here sits the statue of the deified Ramses II together with the triad of Ptah, Amon-Ra and Ra-Harakhti.

It was obvious ever since discovery in the 19th century that nothing in this temple was left to chance and that it was built according to a very precise logic and pre-established plan.

François Champollion was the first of several scholars to note what has become known as the "miracle of the sun". Abu Simbel was built along a pre-determined axis: twice a year, corresponding to the equinoxes, the rising sun penetrates the heart of the mountain and illuminates the statues in the sanctuary. The first rays of the sun follow the axis of the temple precisely, crossing its entire length and gradually flooding the statues of Amon, Ra-Harakhti and the pharaoh in light.

It takes about twenty minutes for the light to pass, yet remarkably Ptah is never struck by the sun's rays: Ptah is, in fact, the god of darkness and the dead.

The Nubian prisoners whom the pharaoh had triumphantly conquered are portrayed on the base of one of the colossi at Abu Simbel.

Portrayed in this magnificent gold ring, now in the Louvre Museum in Paris, are the two valiant horses that took part in the battle of Kadesh with Ramses, "Victory at Thebes" and "Mut is happy". The pharaoh swore to record that memorable day as follows, " ... I personally will undertake to be present every day when they are given their forage ... in the midst of the battle it was they who were there to save me ... it was they who fought beside me...".

KADESH – SUMMER 1275 BC

Although Seti I, Ramses' father, had conquered the Hittites at Kadesh, the victory had not been sufficiently decisive and in the spring of the fifth year of his reign, Ramses decided to resolve the thorny problem of Syria once and for all. First he reinforced the army adding a fourth division to the three already existing: Amon, Ptah, Ra and Seth, each consisting of 5,000 men. His personal guard was formed by "Sherden", "warriors from the sea without masters", probably pirates from the coasts of Asia Minor. Ramses' army was equipped with war chariots that the Egyptians had inherited from the invasion of Hyksos and had then skillfully improved making them speedier and lighter. The cart had a charioteer and soldier with bow and arrow; the harness of the two horses at the neck and breast permitted great ease of handling. With 20,000 men and 200 war chariots, on the ninth day of the second month of summer, 1275 BC, Ramses II moved out of Egypt. Following the same strategy as Tuthmosis III, he followed the Gaza strip as far as Canaan, proceeded through Galilee as far as the source of the Jordan, finally arriving in the broad valley of Bequaa extending between the mountains of Lebanon and the southern reaches of Syria. A month after leaving Egypt, Ramses camped ten kilometres from the city of Kadesh, a Hittite stronghold on the river Orontes. The Hittite king, Muwatalli had created a powerful coalition here with an army of 40,000 men and some 2,500 war chariots. Both sides were aware that the battle of Kadesh would be decisive for control of the entire territory of Syria. The capture of two Bedouin deserters from the Hittite army and their false information regarding the enemy's movements lead Ramses to believe that Muwatalli was more that one hundred kilometres to the north of Kadesh. The pharaoh fell for the trick and with only the Amon division, crossed the river and the forest of Robawi until he was in sight of the city of Kadesh. Unexpectedly the Hittites, who were in fact close to the eastern side of the city, attacked, taking the Ra Division by surprise as it marched directly towards Ramses' camp where he was still discussing the military tactic for the forthcoming battle. While the enemy created confusion and all began to seem lost, the pharaoh threw himself into the fray, leaping onto the chariot with the horseman Menna. Alone, deserted by his soldiers who had been seized by panic, Ramses called on Amon, begging that he would not abandon him and would save his life, "O divine Amon ... You see how I am alone! Are you not my father and am I not your son? I have always done as you have wished ... count the obelisks that I have built in your honour! O Divine Amon, now that I am alone and abandoned by all, my hands and prayers reach out to you. Are you not stronger than a thousand warriors and a thousand heroes?"

And Amon must have heard him, because Ramses – driven by a holy rage – threw himself into the fray wounding and killing numerous enemies, creating confusion in the Hittite ranks and thus making time for the other Egyptian divisions to arrive at the scene of the battle and attack from behind. The Battle of Kadesh also continued the following day and in fact, neither side actually emerged entirely victorious.

The battle was important for two reasons however; firstly because it confirmed Egyptian military power, blocking Hittite expansion, and second because it was the first battle of ancient history to be entirely documented.

The Battle of Kadesh
in the Poem of Pentaur

To portray the pharaoh's victory and triumph over the conquered peoples Egyptian iconography always depicted the king firmly grasping the hair of the captured enemy. Here, at Abu Simbel there are many relief sculptures of Ramses II in this pose and often about to strike the prisoner's head with a strong blow of his sword.

The wall decorations in the Great Temple of Abu Simbel celebrate the military victories of Ramses II. The most interesting and famous is on the north wall where one can follow the various phases of the Battle of Kadesh which concluded the pharaoh's military campaign against the Hittites in the summer of 1275 BC. The *Poem of Pentaur* – though Pentaur was probably not the author, but the scribe who copied it down – is a celebratory, but also objective account of the pharaoh's courage and triumph and recounts with great accuracy the characteristic images of battle: bodies that are fallen and heaped one on top of another, smashed heads, hands chopped off and the pharaoh upright in his chariot, head protected by the "khepresh", a bow held taut by his powerful arm. This long epic poem was engraved in hieroglyphics not only here in Abu Simbel but also on the walls of the temples of Luxor, Karnak, Ramesseum and Derr.

The Small Temple

espite appearances, Abu Simbel is more than a monumental self-glorification of Ramses II. One has only to leave the great temple and turn left towards the temple of Hathor, dedicated by the pharaoh to his wife, Nefertari. The six statues, ten metres tall, each with their left leg set slightly forward, actually seem to emerge from the rock and walk towards the light. Nefertari is represented as Hathor with the horns of the sacred cow, the solar disk and two plumes. The divine consecration of the queen is also celebrated in the delightfully simple interior – an almost square *chamber* with six pilasters in two rows, carved with images of Hathor. Engraved beneath the head of the goddess are stories of Nefertari and Ramses. The walls of this chamber too are decorated with the customary scenes of sacrifice and the massacre of prisoners by the warrior king. The hall leads to a *vestibule* and beyond to the

An overview of the Small Temple of Abu Simbel that the great pharaoh dedicated to his beloved Nefertari in the personification of Hathor.

HATHOR

The origins of the goddess Hathor are extremely ancient. The name means 'The House of Horus'. Usually represented in feminine form, the head of the goddess is surmounted with the horns of a cow. Goddess of love, she was also the patron of music and dance. She was one of the most popular deities of Egypt and was especially venerated in Dendera.

The hypostyle room with the Hathor pillars in which the head of the goddess surmounts he hieroglyphics that tell the story of the king and queen. The deification of Ramses extended to Nefertari whom the king had identified with the local goddess Hathor of Ibhshek, a small Nubian village. It is certain that Nefertari died before this temple was completed, because on the third pillar of the row south of the vestibule she is portrayed as Queen Bent-Anat.

sanctuary where the pharaoh is represented honouring Hathor, identified as his consort. Set between two pillars, and portrayed in the likeness of the sacred cow, the goddess truly seems to stand away from the rock with particularly striking effect. It is impossible not to sense in this small temple a most human and tender act of love for his wife by the great pharaoh.

Small Temple

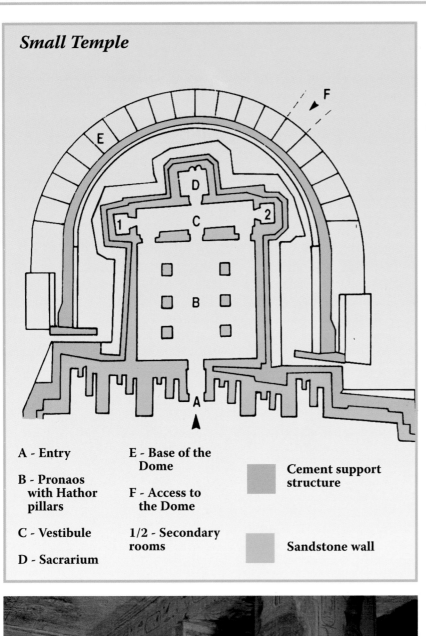

A - Entry

B - Pronaos with Hathor pillars

C - Vestibule

D - Sacrarium

E - Base of the Dome

F - Access to the Dome

1/2 - Secondary rooms

Cement support structure

Sandstone wall

Below, two images of the pillars inside the Small Temple where the head of the goddess is set above hieroglyphics telling the story of the king and queen.

Aswan
The Gateway to Africa

swan (Assuan), the ancient Syene, lies on the right bank of the Nile, 886 kilometres from Cairo. This is where the Valley of the Nile with its typically gentle landscape ends. This is where Egypt ends and Nubia begins. Gone are the farmlands which accompany the bends of the river, replaced now by endless kilometres of desert sands and the majestic still waters of Lake Nasser. The Nile too is transformed and the smooth tranquil waters give way to the sudden troubled waters leaping and eddying around the rocks of the First Cataract.

Trade and barter went on here as early as the third millennium. Nubia, whose ancient name nub (nbw) means "gold", has always been a land of conquest and exploitation. The doorway to Africa, the only communications route between the sea and the heart of the dark continent, Nubia provided the pharaohs with their best soldiers, highly prized woods, precious ivory, perfumed spices, the finest ostrich feathers – as well as gold. Syenite – that pink granite so widely used in Egyptian religious architecture for building temples, and for sculpting colossi and obelisks – came from its many

Feluccas with their large, white sails glide slowly along the waters of the Nile at Aswan.

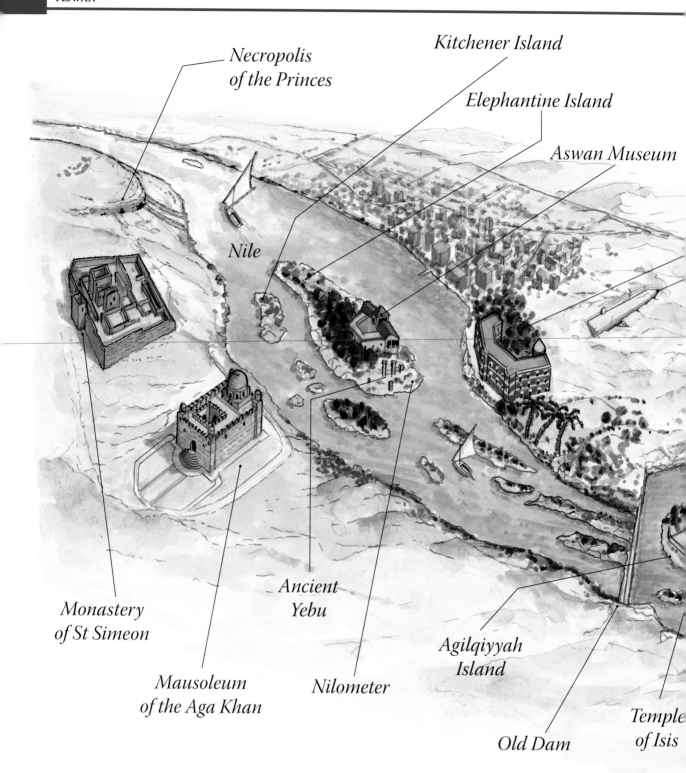

Necropolis
of the Princes

Kitchener Island

Elephantine Island

Aswan Museum

Nile

Monastery
of St Simeon

Mausoleum
of the Aga Khan

Ancient
Yebu

Nilometer

Agilqiyyah
Island

Old Dam

Temple
of Isis

rich quarries. It was so abundant that the quarries were still in use in Roman times. Syene was also of fundamental importance in controlling both the river traffic and that of the desert caravans. The pharaohs maintained an armed garrison there and made Syene the capital of the first nome of Upper Egypt.

In ancient times the Tropic of Capricorn passed through here – over the millennia it has shifted slightly to the south. It was proved by a well: the walls were straight and were il-luminated by the sun only on the day of the summer solstice without any shadows. The Greek scientist, Eratosthenes used it to calculate the circumference of the earth with sur-prising accuracy for his day, around 200 B.C.

In medieval times the city was subject first to the incursions of the Blemi, from Ethiopia, then fell victim to a violent outbreak of the plague. It was gradually abandoned and only began to revive after the Turkish conquest of Egypt. Its modern name derives from the old Egyptian swenet mean-

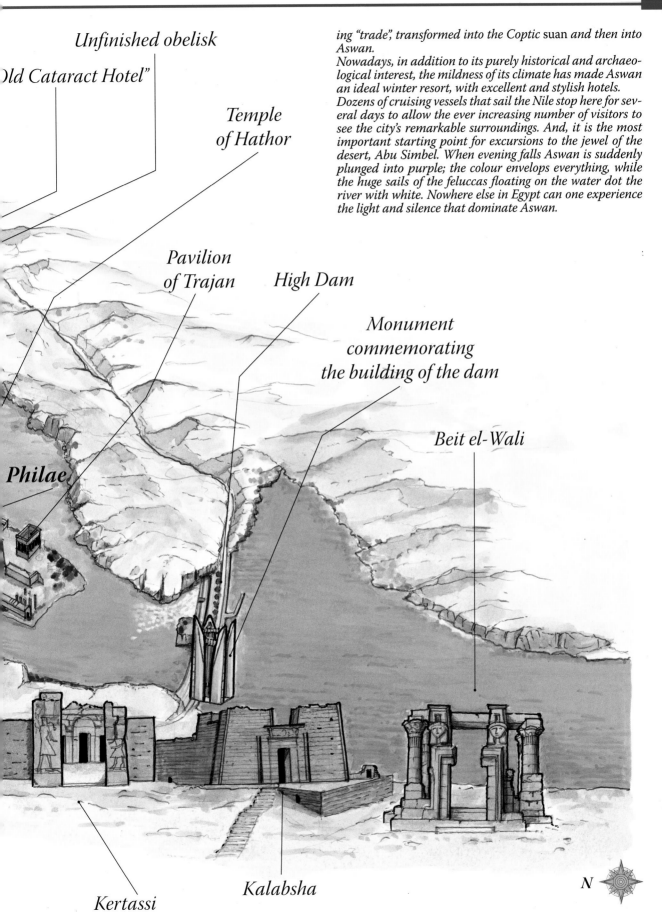

Unfinished obelisk

Old Cataract Hotel"

Temple
of Hathor

Pavilion
of Trajan

High Dam

Monument
commemorating
the building of the dam

Beit el-Wali

Philae

Kertassi

Kalabsha

N

ing "trade", transformed into the Coptic *suan and then into
Aswan.*
*Nowadays, in addition to its purely historical and archaeo-
logical interest, the mildness of its climate has made Aswan
an ideal winter resort, with excellent and stylish hotels.
Dozens of cruising vessels that sail the Nile stop here for several days to allow the ever increasing number of visitors to
see the city's remarkable surroundings. And, it is the most
important starting point for excursions to the jewel of the
desert, Abu Simbel. When evening falls Aswan is suddenly
plunged into purple; the colour envelops everything, while
the huge sails of the feluccas floating on the water dot the
river with white. Nowhere else in Egypt can one experience
the light and silence that dominate Aswan.*

A rock covered with hieroglyphic carvings has been sculpted and eroded by the waters of the Nile.

Elephantine Island

While the rich granite quarries were in ancient *Syene*, most of the trade took place on Elephantine Island. It was here that the governor of the province had his residence, and it was also the centre of the cult of the ram-headed god Khnum. Originally the island was named *Yebu*, which means "elephant" in Egyptian. Gustave Flaubert wrote that the island's women were "the colour of the roasted coffee beans with big maiolica eyes." The island is 1500 metres long and 500 metres wide. It now incorporates two typical Nubian villages and the large "Hotel Assuan Oberoi" as well as the **Aswan Museum** and the **archaeological zone of Yebu**. To land on the island one passes below enormous rocks covered with graffiti and inscriptions dating principally to the 18th (Tuthmosis III and Amenhotep III) and the 26th Dynasties (Psamtik II), docking at the tiny pier constructed of material that was taken from buildings dating to the New Kingdom.

The Bazaar

For atmosphere and charm the bazaar of Aswan in is second only to that of Cairo.

Parallel to the Corniche – the avenue which runs along the Nile, shaded by tall hibiscus trees laden with red flowers – it winds through the narrow streets of the old city. There is a real feel of Africa in the air of this souk: the tall wicker baskets set on the ground are full of exotic spices and enticing brightly coloured powders, from karkade to henne, from saffron pistils to curry, from red pepper to the dark-leafed mint tea. Objects in braided straw, in ebony, in ivory abound. Everywhere a teeming of dark-skinned peoples (the Nubians are thinner and darker than the rest of the Egyptian population) and a fluttering of long white robes.

Feluccas moored in front of the entrance to the Aswan Museum.

On these pages, a gallery of pictures revealing the riches of the collections in the Aswan Museum.

The Aswan Museum

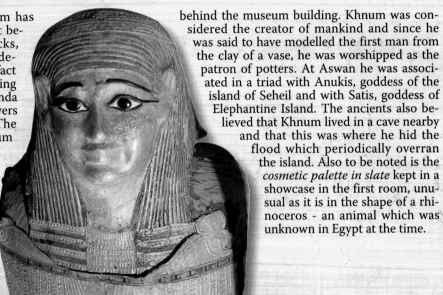

Since 1912 this small museum has been located in the villa that belonged to William Wellicocks, the English engineer who designed the Old Dam of Aswan. In fact it has all the appearance of a charming inviting colonial house, with a veranda opening out onto the garden, flowers and plants growing all around. The archaeological finds in the museum all come from excavations undertaken in Aswan and other sites in Lower Nubia. Of particular interest is the *mummy of the sacred ram* in a gilded sarcophagus. It dates to 330-305 BC and was found in a tomb just behind the museum building. Khnum was considered the creator of mankind and since he was said to have modelled the first man from the clay of a vase, he was worshipped as the patron of potters. At Aswan he was associated in a triad with Anukis, goddess of the island of Seheil and with Satis, goddess of Elephantine Island. The ancients also believed that Khnum lived in a cave nearby and that this was where he hid the flood which periodically overran the island. Also to be noted is the *cosmetic palette in slate* kept in a showcase in the first room, unusual as it is in the shape of a rhinoceros - an animal which was unknown in Egypt at the time.

Nilometer

"*T*here are marks which measure the height of the water for irrigation. They are used by the farmers to measure the flow of the water, while the state officials use it to establish the amount of taxes. In fact, the higher the water the higher the taxes". This is what Strabo once wrote about the Nilometer, a staircase of 90 steps which descended into the waters of the Nile and made it possible to know in advance the date of the flood and the amount of water, thanks to a graduated scale engraved on its walls. The inscriptions are in Greek (a scale with Arab measurements was added later) and record some of the famous floods, from Augustus up to Septimius Severus.

The Nilometer, with the steps leading down to the river and the markings cut into the walls. As the water rose along the steps it was possible determine the flow and forecast the magnitude of the flood.

Ancient Yebu

*F*urther on, beyond the Nilometer, is what remains of the ancient city of Abu. The main building was the **temple dedicated to Khnum**, begun in the 30th Dynasty under Nectanebo II and continued under the Ptolemies and the Romans. It consisted of a court behind which was the *hypostyle hall* and the *sanctuary*. We can still see a large *portal* in granite with cartouches of Alexander Aegos and a *naos*, also of grey granite, with the pharaoh Nectanebo II worshipping Khnum. In the vicinity, the **small temple of Heka-ib** also came to light. Heka-ib was a nomarch at the end of the Old Kingdom to whom his successors dedicated this small temple that consists of a court surrounded by *naos-chapels*, each of which contained a statue of Heka-ib. Even further towards the southernmost tip of the island stands another *chapel* of the Ptolemaic period rebuilt by using material found in Kalabsha when the temple there was dismantled.

Below and facing page, above, the luxurious "Old Cataract Hotel" at Aswan, in perfect colonial style opened its doors in 1899 and was the meeting point for the elite during the English colonial period. It was one of Agatha Christie's favourite hotels and indeed, some scenes of the film Death on the Nile were shot here.

Kitchener Island

Nubian Villages

North of Elephantine is the Island of Trees, better known as Kitchener Island. Lord Horatio Kitchener was an English general who had fought valiantly in the Sudan in 1898, defeating the army of the Mahadi. Consul General in Egypt, he fell in love with this island set in the middle of the Nile, where he could fully indulge his passion for exotic flowers and plants. This splendid botanical garden contains the rarest examples from Africa and Asia: a symphony of colours and fragrances accompanies us on our leisurely wanderings along shady avenues. Bougainvilleas and poinsettias, hibiscus and clematis, mangoes and sycamores. Fragrances that are pungent or subtle, shades of colour ranging from brilliant reds to delicate pinks. Birds also love this enchanted garden and live here undisturbed among the bushes and the undergrowth. In the southern part of the island, a tiny bay populated by white ducks has been created under a lovely terrace.

Immersed in the green of the palm groves on Elephantine Island, three Nubian villages appear quite suddenly transporting us into a different world. Here the inhabitants are extremely courteous and are always ready to offer the visitor a cup of fragrant mint tea. The houses are brightly coloured in green, blue and yellow. Often the black cube of Mecca, the sacred *Kaaba*, is painted on the exterior, a sign that the owner of the house had made a pilgrimage to the holy city of Mecca. Sometimes the means of transportation is also painted – a plane, a ship, a car...

Left, lush vegetation on Kitchener Island, and, below, a typical Nubian village.

The Nubia Museum

*T*he result of the fruitful cooperation between UNESCO and the Egyptian Government, the Nubia Museum at Aswan may be considered the final, and successful consequence of the formation of Lake Nasser and the international mobilization that embraced the cause of saving the vestiges of a culture – the Nubian in fact – that risked losing its roots and history, completely and for ever. In the nineteen eighties the pressing need to find a suitable home for the hundreds of objects that had been taken to safety from tombs, temples and ancient settlements which deserved to be known by the world became acutely felt. A special committee was established to study the matter and that was how the idea of creating a museum was born. It was to be a museum in an appropriate environmental setting, easily reachable by visitors and yet an integral part of the completely Nubian panorama, close to the Nile (and also to the hotel district)), nestled in the rocky cradle that has always been the background of the city of Aswan. Nearly 20 years later, in November 1997, the museum housed in a building

Views of the museum with its simple exterior built in typical Nubian style and surrounded by a splendid garden, and just a few of the splendid objects inside the museum.

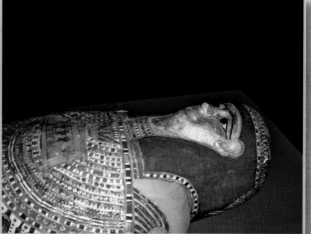

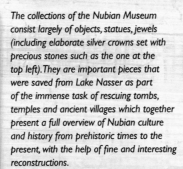

The collections of the Nubian Museum consist largely of objects, statues, jewels (including elaborate silver crowns set with precious stones such as the one at the top left). They are important pieces that were saved from Lake Nasser as part of the immense task of rescuing tombs, temples and ancient villages which together present a full overview of Nubian culture and history from prehistoric times to the present, with the help of fine and interesting reconstructions.

designed by architect Mahmoud al-Hakim of Egypt, according to the architectural canons of Nubian villages, with small apertures suited to the hot climate, became reality. It has 50,000 square metres of exhibition space, of which only 7,000 are enclosed within the three story museum building and 43,000 outdoors, making it an extraordinary open air museum, where among other things a typical Nubian house was reconstructed down to the smallest details, and a sort of cave was set up as the appropriate home for some prehistoric items. The museum's rich and interesting collections make it possible to travel through Nubian history in its entirety, from the prehistoric period to the pharaonic, from, the Greco-Roman era to the Christian era and to Islam with specific theme areas devoted to the main events and most important stages, a constant eye focused on the development of the traditions and culture of the Nubian people. There are also many var-

ied temporary exhibitions that are held to bear witness to the great vitality of this new institution which in the coming years will continue to grow still with the patronage of the Egyptian Government and under the aegis of UNESCO.

Mausoleum of the Aga Khan

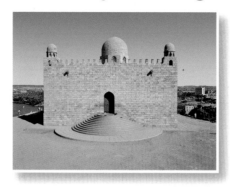

*I*n 1957 the Aga Khan III Mohammed Shah, spiritual head of the Ismailian Muslims, died. This community, whose centre is in India, has about four million followers, scattered throughout the world.

Extremely rich, (in 1946, in Bombay, according to tradition, made him a gift of his weight in diamonds – 105 kg!), he used to spend part of the winter in the villa on the left bank of the Nile. As stated in his will, two years after his death the Aga Khan was buried here, in the mausoleum called the Begum built above the white house. The mausoleum was built in pink limestone, on the model of the Cairo mosque of El-Guyushi, in the unadorned Fatimid style. Inside, the tomb is of white Carrara marble, with inscriptions from the Koran round the walls, so beautifully engraved they look like embroidery. His beloved wife, the legendary Begum, née Yvette Labrousse, Miss France of 1930 has been resting beside him since July 2000. When Begum lived in the villa below the mausoleum, one red rose was placed in front of the tomb every day.

Two views of the Mausoleum of the Aga Khan: delicate pink sandstone stands out against the rocks and gardens below.

An overview of the Monastery of Saint Simeon; right, the central chapel of the apse with fragments of frescoes in which we can recognize Christ Pantokrator.

Monastery of St Simeon

Once, cultivated fields covered this small valley right up to the Nile. Today the imposing ruins of this monastery, a genuine fortress, are set against the savage beauty of the desert.

The *Deir Amba Samaan* (as it is called in Arab) is one of the largest and best preserved Coptic monasteries in all of Egypt. Following the death of bishop Hadra, it was built between the 6th and 8th centuries. It could house up to 300 monks and offer shelter to many hundreds of pilgrims. After existing for almost five hundred years, it was destroyed by the Arabs in 1321, when many of the monks were killed and the survivors were driven out. The surrounding wall of stone and unbaked brick flanked by towers ten metres high lend it a majestic and solemn air which inspires respect and awe. Inside, the convent was designed like a real city in miniature. On the first level is the tripartite *church* with an apse with three chapels. Traces of frescoes depicting *Christ Pantokrator* and twenty-four *seated saints* are still visible. Above each saint a letter of the Coptic alphabet is painted. A staircase leads to the second floor, where the real monastery is, with a long corridor onto which the monks' *cells* face, and the service rooms for the community, such as kitchen, bakery, cellar, are situated. If we climb to the top of the walls, the desert stretches before us in all its majesty. All around is sand, with camels slowly crossing it to bring visitors here. At the end of the valley we are struck by the stunning contrast of Aswan overlooking the blue waters of the Nile and the white feluccas lazily waiting, half hidden in the green of the palm groves. It is particularly lovely to approach the monastery at sunset, when the ruins take on a rosy hue that blends with the sand from which they seem to emerge as if by magic.

Necropolis of the Princes

The left bank of the Nile is dominated by the hill called *Qubett el Hawa* (the "summit of the winds") with a small ruined temple offering an unforgettable spectacle of Aswan, the mass of rocks which form the First Cataract and the desert all around. Immediately below, are about forty tombs that go to make up the interesting necropolis of the princes of Elephantine. Contemporaries of the last pharaohs of the Old Kingdom, these dignitaries had their tombs dug into the rock. Entrance was via a steep ramp which served to haul the sarcophagus. The layout of the tomb is generally very schematic: a rectangular chamber with pillars, the chapel and the sarcophagus room. The decoration is also extremely simple and consists only of paintings, as the limestone in which the tomb was cut was not suitable for relief sculpture.

Tomb of Heka-ib

Discovered in 1947, this tomb belonged to Heka-ib, a dignitary about whom we know only that he was governor of Elephantine at the end of the Old Kingdom, during the 6th Dynasty. Though he seems to have been popular, his success was posthumous as, for a reason that is unknown to us, he was deified and the small temple already seen on Elephantine Island near the temple of Khnum was erected in his honour. His tomb is not large nor does it have any outstanding decoration. When it was discovered, however, about sixty *steles* dedicated to him were found in the court.

Tombs of Mehu and Sabni

These two tombs at the southernmost end of the necropolis are intercommunicating for their owners were father and son. Mehu, "hereditary prince" and "only friend" during the 6th Dynasty, had travelled as far south as the Second Cataract and during the journey encountered death. His son Sabni, as can be read on the sides of the entrance to the second tomb, organized an expedition to go in search of his father's body and bring it back home where solemn funeral rites were celebrated, with expert embalmers called in to mummify him. Mehu's tomb has a vast hall with three rows of six columns each. At the centre

The exterior of the tomb of Mehu and Sabni.

between two pillars is a block of granite which served as an offering table: to be noted are the symbols for bread and the drainage canals for the ritual libations. Sabni's tomb is divided by twelve pillars arranged in two rows and is decorated with scenes of hunting and fishing.

Tomb of Sirenput I
Very little remains of this tomb, in which the son of Satethotep, a 12th-Dynasty prince at the time of Amenemhet II was buried, to indicate that it was the largest and most richly endowed tomb in the entire necropolis. Even so, part of the enclosure and the entrance portal in limestone still exist, with fine bas-reliefs depicting the deceased

prince, the "Superior of the prophets of Satis". The façade of the tomb had a portico with six piers. The interior consisted of a chamber with four pilasters which must originally have been richly decorated with paintings though now in very poor condition: the scenes referred to daily life on land and sea.

Tomb of Sirenput II
The tomb, one of the best preserved, belonged to the "Superior of the prophets of Khnum" during the 12th Dynasty. It consisted of a first chamber with six pillars, a gallery flanked by six niches each of which contained the mummy-like statue of the deceased prince, and a

Above, the tomb of Sirenput I; right one of the decorations on the tomb of Sirenput II, with the prince and his son in front of a table richly laden with offerings.

second square chamber with four pillars, each of which was decorated with a lovely image of Sirenput. This is followed by the back chapel which is painted: the prince is shown with his small son rendering him homage before a table set with bread, sweets, fruit, even a duck and bunches of grapes. The adjacent wall is decorated with the figure of the wife of the prince, who was a priestess of Hathor, also shown seated before a prepared table.

The unfinished obelisk

*I*f this obelisk had been finished it would have been a candidate for the *Guinness Book of Records*. It would in fact have been over 41 metres high with a base of four metres and consequently a weight of 1,267 tons! But a crack in the granite, perhaps the result of a tremor, or the poor quality of the stone, brought the work to a halt and the obelisk remained as we see it now, abandoned on the ground near those granite quarries which reveal much about how the ancient Egyptians cut stone. Once the ancient quarries of Aswan stretched for more than six kilometres from the Nile. This was the stone the Egyptians favoured for the facing their pyramids, and since it was near the river, the stone could easily be loaded onto boats and carried upstream.

The incisions cut regularly into the rock provide indications of how the blocks of stone were quarried. Wooden wedges or quoins were inserted into these grooves, which indicated the surface to be extracted and these were then soaked with water. As the wood expanded, the quoins burst, splitting off the rock in the desired direction, with surfaces that were relatively smooth and ready for polishing.

Opposite page, above, the unfinished obelisk seen from the top.
Opposite page, below, and this page, above, two period photos documenting
the immense amount of work that went into building the dam that made it possible
to irrigate a huge expanse of land.

The Dams of Aswan

*A*bout five kilometres south of the city the course of the Nile is crossed by the Old Dam of Aswan (*Es Saad*, the dam), built by the English between 1898 and 1902 with an initial height of 30.5 metres and a capacity of a billion cubic metres of water. Before long this proved insufficient and in two stages (from 1907 to 1912 and from 1929 to 1934) the dam was enlarged to its present size: 41.5 metres high and with a capacity of five billion cubic metres of water. Still this was not enough to meet the requirements of the Egyptian territory. The drama of Egypt is to be found in two numbers: 900,000 square kilometres of land of which only 38,000, not much more than 4%, can be cultivated. A new dam would not only increase the amount of farmland, but irrigation would become a reality and the annual production of electricity would be increased. It was thus decided to embark upon the construction of a new barrier, called the "barrier against hunger", a new

MAP OF THE TWO ASWAN DAMS

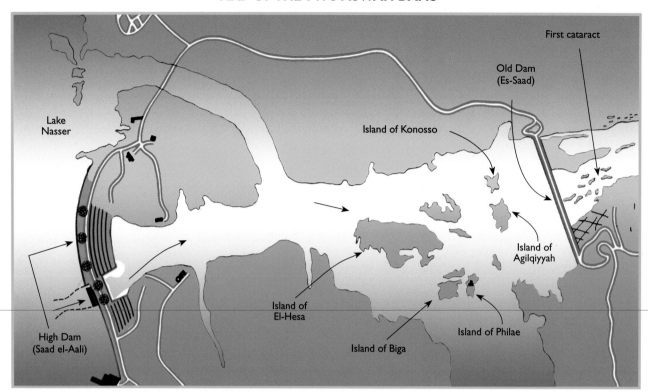

CROSS SECTION OF THE HIGH DAM

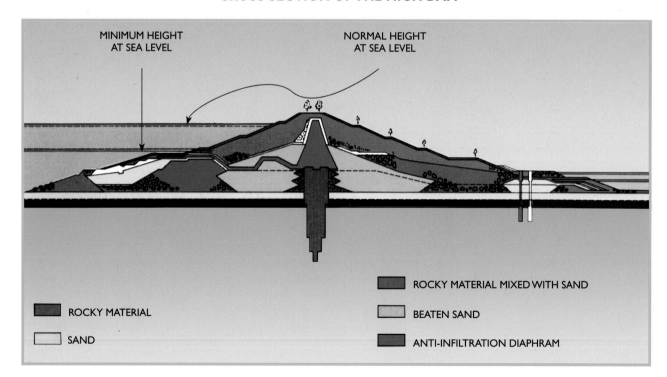

dam which, as Nasser said, "would set Egypt on the road to modernity".

The High Dam (*Saad el Aali*) is about eight kilometres upstream from the Old Dam. The Soviet Union was entrusted with the study of the project. Construction began in January 1960; on May 14, 1964 the waters of the Nile were deviated into a branch canal and in 1972 the work – of vast dimensions – could be considered finished. The body of water thus formed, Lake Nasser, is 500 kilometres long (150 of which are in Sudanese territory) and has a capacity of 157 billion cubic metres of water: second only to the dam of Kariba on the Zambesi River.

The creation of this artificial basin obviously brought about radical modifications in the landscape and in the environment. First of all, the numerous Nubian villages in the area involved had to be evacuated. Then attention was centred on the dramatic situation of the many important archaeological sites in Nubia which would inevitably have been submerged. When it was realized that the economic improvement of Egypt meant the irreparable destruction of its archaeological heritage, UNESCO reacted to the call for aid launched by the Egyptian and Sudanese governments and set in motion a gigantic campaign to raise the funds needed to save the threatened temples. Not one of the fourteen temples involved has been preserved on its original site: once dismantled, they have been faithfully reconstructed elsewhere.

Among these, the temple of **Kalabsha**, clearly visible from the High Dam, is one of the finest and best preserved.

The stylized lotus blossom monument erected to commemorate the labours of those who worked on the pharaonic-scale project of building the Aswan Dam.

PHILAE
the "pearl of Egypt"

*I*n the midst of a fascinating landscape of granite rocks, the sacred island, domain of the goddess Isis, raises its columns and pillars towards the cloudless sky, giving one the impression of being in a purely imaginary place. The temple of Philae is one of the three best preserved Ptolemaic temples, the other two being those of Edfu and Dendera.

Philae was the largest of the three islands at the south end of the group of rocks that comprise the First Cataract, and is 400 metres long and 135 metres wide. The name

These pictures show the extraordinary majesty of the temple of Isis on Agilqiyyah island with its two impressive pylons and magnificent fabric of reliefs and decorations.

itself reveals its unique geographic position: Pilak in fact, as it was called in the ancient texts, meant "the corner island" or "the end island". For originally Philae was on the east bank of the Nile, in the corner of a small bay, and also at the southernmost tip of the First Cataract. Of the other two islets, **Bigah** (today partially submerged) was particularly sacred for it was Osiris' place of eternal sleep and therefore out of bounds to all human beings. Only priests who came by boat from Philae were allowed there to celebrate their sacred rites on the 360 offering tables which indicated where Osiris was buried. The temples on Philae were dedicated to his bride Isis who with the force of her love had recomposed his scattered limbs and resuscitated him. The cult of the goddess on this island dates to extremely ancient times and it was a tradition that at least once a year Egyptians should go on pilgrimage to the sacred island. It was not until AD 535, under the reign of Justinian, that the priests dedicated to the cult were removed.

The third islet is **Agilqiyyah**: and this is where we can now admire the temple complex which was originally on Philae, barely 500 metres away.

The sacred island, in fact, was above water throughout the year until 1898. With the construction of the Old

Philae, sacred to Isis and her temple was always a fascinating destination for pilgrims and travellers. On these pages, a historic photo and a lovely drawing by David Roberts (below) have consigned the solemn atmosphere that pervades these sites to eternity.

Dam, it remained submerged by the artificial lake most of the year. Only in August and September when the lock-gates of the dam were opened to alleviate the pressure of the flood waters, did the island emerge so it could be visited. The construction of the High Dam put Philae in a critical situation: the sacred island would have found itself in a closed basin in which the waters, no longer twenty metres high as before but only four, would have created a continual ebb and flow that, with the passing of the years, would have inevitably eroded the foundations of the temples which sooner or later would have collapsed. Thus, between 1972 and 1980, they were dismantled and rebuilt on this islet (where the topography of Philae was recreated) in a position that was higher above the waters of the lake. The temple complex includes the **pavilion of Nectanebo**, the monumental **temple of Isis** with its annexes, the charming **pavilion of Trajan** and the **small Hathor temple**.

Plate XVI of Rosellini's "Religious Monuments" shows a copy of the scenes painted on the walls of the Temple of Isis on Philae.
The upper register shows the Abaton (from the Greek abaton "inaccessible [place]", that corresponds to the Egyptian At wabt, "pure place"). During the Greco-Roman era the name was attributed to many places of worship scattered through the country where it was believed that various parts of the body of Osiris were buried.
Right, the rock represents the Cataract of the Nile: above a crocodile is the body of Osiris, with Harpocrates and Atum in the tondo.
Left, the goddess Isis in front of the doors leading to the Abaton. If the most important tomb of Osiris was located at Abidos, the best documented is this one on the island of Bigah.
Classical writers such as Plutarch, Strabo, Seneca and Diodorus have left us descriptions of the religious rituals that were practiced here.

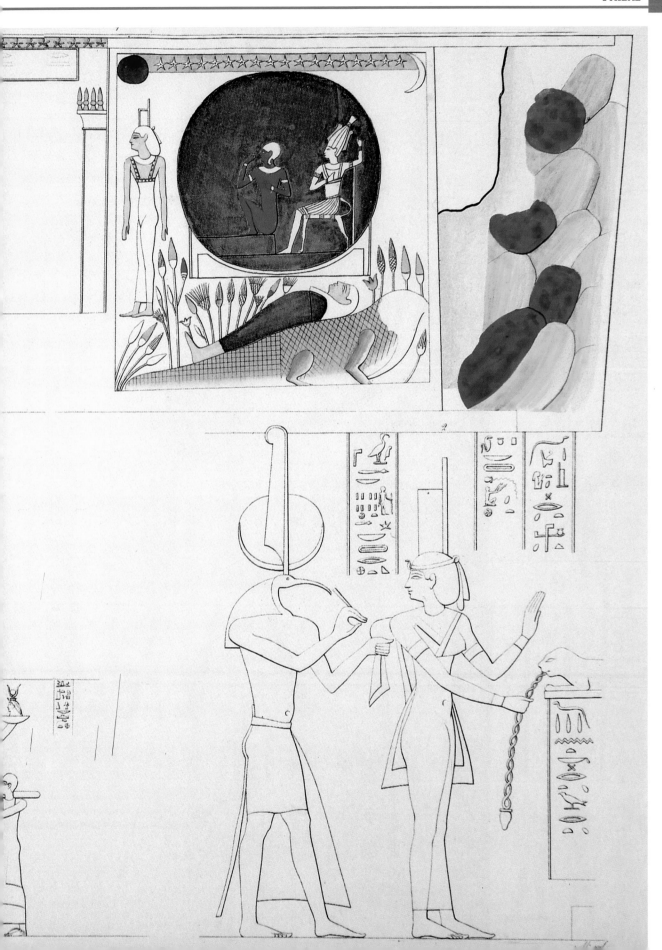

Temple of Isis

The landing-stage for the boats that bring tourists to visit the complex of Philae lies at the southwest tip of the island.

The first building to be encountered is the **pavilion of Nectanebo I**, a rectangular portico with fourteen bell columns and Hathor capitals: here the broad face of the goddess also has the ears of a cow (fairly common in all later capitals) so that it also represents the form of a sistrum, the fa-vourite musical instrument of Isis, and also a symbol of Ihi, Hathor's young son. The pavilion dates to the 4th century B.C. and is therefore considered the oldest temple in the complex. In front is the large *dromos*, with porticoes on either side. The one on the right was never finished; the one on the left has 32 columns with traces of decoration on the ceiling and offering scenes on the columns and the back wall. The plant-shaped capitals differ one from the other.

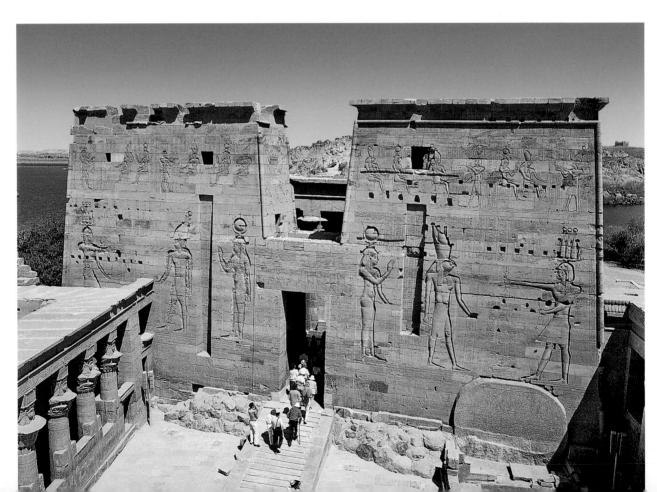

The view is now majestically completed by the temple of Isis with its monumental *first pylon*: it is 18 metres high and 45.5 metres wide and consists of two massive towers which flank the portal. On the tower the pharaoh Ptolomy XI Neos Dionysos grasps, in customary pose, his prisoners by the hair and prepares to sacrifice them to the gods Isis, Horus and Hathor. In the left tower, the reliefs which show the pharaoh armed with a staff and about to kill the enemy prisoners are in poorer condition. Passing between the two pylons, under the portal built by Nectanebo I whose cartouches can be seen, we find on the right a relief commemorating the French victory over the Mamelukes in the "an VII de la République" (1799). We are now in the temple *court* with the back wall formed by the second pylon and the right by a porticoed building with various annexes used by the priests. The elegant mammisi temple on the left side is a peripteral building (surrounded on four sides by columns with capitals terminating in Hathor sistrums), with three rooms preceded by a pronaos. Isis and her son Horus, whose birth, childhood and education are narrated in the fine decorations, were worshipped in the **mammisi**. Also to be noted above on the outer façade, the reproduction of the text of the Rosetta stone which made it possible to decipher Egyptian hieroglyphics. The *second pylon* (22 metres high and 32 wide) is higher than but not exactly parallel to the first. On the façade it also has the customary scene of Pharaoh Ptolemy XI Neos Dionysos massacring the prisoners before the gods. On the right, an enormous block of granite commemorates a donation of

More pictures of the Temple of Isis, opposite page an aerial view of the second pylon (below) and the massive colonnade of the dromos (above). Right, at Philae a detail of one of the Hathor capitals of the bell columns on the elegant pavilion of Nectanebo I.

lands that Ptolemy VI made to the temple. A few steps lead to the *hypostyle hall*, with ten columns with polychrome floral capitals and traces of decoration on the ceiling: symbols of Upper and Lower Egypt, sun boats, astronomical symbols. In the 6th century at the time of the bishop Theodorus, the pronaos was transformed into a Christian church as witnessed by the many Coptic crosses engraved on the walls. From here access is gained to the *naos*, which consists of twelve rooms and a crypt, all decorated with liturgical scenes. After this came the *sanctuary*, containing the boat with the image of the goddess. A staircase leads to the terrace where a vestibule and a chamber comprise the *funerary chapel of Osiris*: the decoration narrates the Osiris cycle with the death, funeral and magical rites and the resurrection of the god.

While most of the decorations at Philae regard sacred rites and tributes to the gods, there is one that stands out for its originality and the quite atypical subject represented. This is the *gate or bastion of Hadrian*, an aedicule that dates to Antonine times and that is situated in the western wing of the temple of Isis, on a level with the second pylon. Inside the gate, on the north wall, a *relief* sculpture illustrates the Egyptian concept of the source of the Nile. In fact Hapy, the deification of the Upper and Lower Nile, is shown in an anthropomorphic and hermaphroditic form. The god is shown in a cave surrounded by a serpent and he holds two vases from which water flows. In fact, the ancient Egyptians believed that the source of the Nile was in the neighbourhood of the First Cataract near a mountain called Mu Hapy (meaning "water of Hapy"). The annual rites in honour of the god were celebrated by the pharaoh himself and began in the middle of June when the star Sotis marked the beginning of the river's flood.

On the other side – on the right side of the temple of Isis – is another jewel of this great Ptolemaic complex of Philae: **Trajan's pavilion**. Overlooking the river, extremely elegant and finely proportioned, it has in a sense become the symbol of the entire island. In olden times this was where the sacred barge with the statue of Isis landed during the magnificent processions on the river. Rebuilt by the emperor Trajan, the rectangu-

Left, the structure known as the gate of Hadrian.

Opposite page, the small hypostyle room that precedes the entrance to the sanctuary of Isis shown still gleaming with brilliant decorations, by David Roberts.

The elegant Pavilion of Trajan that stands next to the temple on the island of Agilqiyyah and a detail of a column with an elaborately carved capital.

lar kiosk has fourteen columns with bell capitals and screen walls, two of which are decorated with scenes representing Trajan making offerings to Isis, Osiris and Horus.

Beyond the kiosk is the **small temple of Hathor**, erected by Ptolemy VI Philometer and Euergetes II, but decorated later by Augustus. Some of the reliefs are rather amusing and show, among other things, a priest playing the double flute and some monkeys dancing while one plays the lute.

Philae represents a perfect synthesis of the Egyptian, Greek and Roman civilizations: here architecture and design are one. It should be remembered that once, before the waters of the Old Dam washed them clean, all the capitals were painted in brilliant colours – blue, red, yellow and green – as is seen in the paintings of those travellers who saw them before the temple was submerged in the artificial basin of Aswan. Despite the fact that all the original colour has disappeared, Philae remains that masterpiece of grace and enchantment, as Amelia Edwards wrote, a marvellous example of elegance and charm, which led Pierre Loti to call it the "pearl of Egypt".

Kalabsha

Kalabsha was the ancient *Talmis*, the most important city of the Dodecaschenum ("Land of the twelve miles"), and was situated about forty kilometres south of its present site. The god Mandulis was worshipped there – his head surmounted by a complicated diadem – identified with Horus by the Egyptians. In importance and size, the **sanctuary** dedicated to this local god was second only to Abu Simbel. Seventy-one metres long and thirty-five wide, it was defined by the English writer Amelia Edwards as the "Karnak of Nubia". Of the "inner sanctuary" type, the temple was built on an earlier one from the time of Amenophis II. The plan includes a pylon, a court, a pronaos and a naos formed by three successive chambers. The *pylon* is 41 metres high and it is possible to climb to the top to admire the beautiful panorama of the High Dam and Lake Nasser. The pylon leads to the paved *court* 20 metres long, where worshippers had access during the great festivals. It is surrounded on three sides by a porch and columns which collapsed when an earthquake struck but which were partially reconstructed when the temple was recomposed. Then comes the *pronaos* which had twelve columns with bell capitals. The façade is decorated with numerous inscriptions. One, in Greek, narrates how Silco, king of Ethiopia in the middle of the 6th century AD, had come to destroy Talmis, inhabited by his enemies. Another inscription, also in Greek, notes the decree issued by the governor Aurelio Besarione who, around the year 250, ordered on religious grounds that all the swineherds and their pigs had to leave the temple within fifteen days. The interior of the pronaos is also decorated with figures of Mandulis, Thoth, Horus, etc. Until the late 19th century, the decorations still had their original colours. Nowadays, unfortunately, all trace has been lost and we must trust in the descriptions and drawings of travellers in the past who were lucky enough to see and copy them. After the pronaos come the three chambers which formed the *naos*, each one lower than the one before, and with columns supporting the ceiling. In the *cell* which contained the statue of Mandulis, interesting decorations, characterized by a certain freshness of execution, have survived.

Only the first of the original encircling walls of the temple still exists. A sort of spacious sentry corridor, which also contains a *Nilometer*, is set between the stone wall and that of the temple. To the west, on the external wall, is an enormous relief sculpture of Mandulis: he is shown twice, on the right in his human aspect and on the left in his divine aspect.

At the time of the great rescue of the Nubian temples, technicians of the German Federal Republic were responsible for Kalabsha and, after dismantling it into 13,000 blocks they rebuilt it on this promontory, a stone sentinel for the endless expanse of Lake Nasser.

Above, relief carving of the human-headed bird symbolizing "Ba" the spiritual element usually translated as "soul." It is often portrayed giving the mummy of the deceased the breath of life. In this relief at Kalabsha it wears a complex royal crown on its head.

Two views of the hypostyle and the massive pylon of Kalabsha. From the first room of the sanctuary is possible to access the roof of the temple that offers a magnificent view of the surroundings where the temples of Kertassi and Beit el-Wali were reconstructed.

Kertassi

Erected on high ground above the Nile, the **small temple** of Kertassi was dedicated to Isis and originally stood in the town of *Tzitzis*. It was moved and only partially rebuilt on the current site, south of the Temple of Kalabsha, during the nineteen sixties. It was very similar and probably contemporary, to Trajan's Pavilion at Philae, rectangular in shape with columns and composite capitals decorated with plant motifs, joined by screen walls and with two large Hathor pillars at the portal. Damaged by an earthquake even prior to the move, the temple of Kertassi must have been deeply scarred by time and the elements. Only one of the architraves which once supported the roof – which no longer exists – remains now and it is covered with numerous inscriptions.

Some details of the reconstructed small of Kertassi with its fine Hathor capitals on which Hathor is portrayed with the ears of a cow, the animal sacred to the goddess.

Beit el-Wali

The **rock-cut temple** of Beit el-Wali is not far from the large temple of Kalabsha. The name means "House of the Governor" and it was built by the viceroy of Kush (Upper Nubia) for Ramses II. It is a *speos* cut into the mountain and consists of only two chambers, a long hall and the *sanctuary*, both preceded by an open court, the walls of which are decorated in relief with military scenes that commemorate the victorious campaigns of Ramses II: over Syria and Libya on the right wall and over Ethiopia on the left. The vestibule, which was transformed into a church in the 6th century, has two proto-Doric columns supporting the ceiling: here the bas-reliefs of religious scenes still have their original colours fairly well preserved. Ramses II is shown before the falcon-headed Horus and Selkis, and the pharaoh is also seen making offerings to the holy triad of Khnum, Satis and Anukis.

The courtyard leading to the rock-carved temple of Beit el-Wali, on the right wall the portrayal of Ramses II's victory over the Syrians and Libyans.

*Plate LXIV in Rosellini's "Historical Monuments" shows the pharaoh about to strike
an Ethiopian prisoner with his sword to symbolize his victory over the Africans as described in
the text at the side. A symmetrical scene portrays the pharaoh striking an Asian enemy
to commemorate his victory over those peoples.*

Island of Seheil

Upstream, a few kilometres from Aswan, is the First Cataract of the Nile, a vast zone of turbulent waters and whirlpools with innumerable rocks and islets. Seen from above, the cataract really looks like primordial chaos. River traffic was interrupted here: the boats unloaded their camels which went round the rocks carrying the goods, and then sailed on greatly lightened, thus passing with ease through the narrow passages formed by the islets. The pharaoh Sesostris III, in the 12th Dynasty, had a canal dug parallel to the river to allow the ships to continue their journey towards the farthest parts of Nubia.

Travellers, soldiers, merchants: all left traces of their journey in dozens and dozens of graffiti which cover the black granite on Seheil. The island was sacred to Anukis, represented in female form and with plumes on her head, and to whom a *temple* that is no longer exists was dedicated. All that is left are the remains of two other **small temples**, one from the time of Amenophis II (18th dynasty) and the other from the time of Ptolemy XIV Philopator. There are about two hundred inscriptions on the island, and they range from the 6th Dynasty to the Ptolemaic period. The most interesting is no. 81, known also as the *"famine stele"* of the Ptolemaic period. It refers to the terrible famine which had smitten Egypt for seven years and how the pharaoh Djoser thanked Khnum with the erection of a temple because the god had finally sent a flood of the Nile plain. The text of this stele made it possible to identify Djoser as the pharaoh who had the step pyramid in Saqqara built.

On these pages, fascinating views of some of the nearly 200 inscriptions that dot the rocks on the Island of Seheil.

CULTURE HELPING HISTORY

In 1963, as we have seen, in order to avoid destruction by the waters of Lake Nasser, some temples were dismantled or removed, transported to a safer location and rebuilt – though some were taken from their original site and entirely reconstructed in the countries that had assisted in their preservation. Thus it is that today, in Turin we can visit the temple of El-Lesiya, dedicated to Horus and Satet, originally located 200 kilometres from Aswan; in Madrid we find the massive temple of Dabod dedicated to Isis, that once stood 15 kilometres from Philae; in the Netherlands, at Leiden is the temple of Taffeh dedicated to Amun and Isis, originally 40 kilometres from Philae, and in New York is the temple of Dendur, built at the time of Augustus 77 kilometres from Philae, dedicated to the brothers Peteese and Pihar who were deified. Other temples instead were relocated closer to their original site, thus remaining in Lower Nubia or in Egypt. Three great temples have been rebuilt on the banks of the vast Lake Nasser: Wadi al-Sabu, Dakkah and Maharraqah. Other temples have been located 60 kilometres from here, such as Amadah and Derr, as well as the tomb of Penniut, governor of Uauat during the reign of Ramses VI.

Rocks and ancient ruins, including those of the still majestic fortress of Qasr Ibrahim, characterize the shores of Lake Nasser.

Dakkah

Dedicated to the god Thoth, the **temple** of Dakkah was built in the Ptolemaic and Roman periods. Facing rather unusually to the north, the building stood 40 km. to the north of its present site, about 1 km. to the north east of the temple of Ramses II. On the west bank of the Nile, Dakkah is the precise location where a temple dedicated to Selqet, an ancient scorpion goddess, once stood. Inscriptions found on blocks of stone that were reused tell us that king Amon-Emhat IV of the 12th dynasty had built the temple on this site; Thutmosis III, Seti I and Merneptah left their names in the sanctuary that had been modified. The lofty and regular structure that we see today dates from the Ptolemaic period; the original nucleus consisted of a stone portal, *courtyard* and a *chapel* which had a vaulted ceiling, an atrium, two vestibules and a cella. The nucleus was created by Ptolemy IV Philopator and the Meorite king Ergamenes, his subject. In 146 BC Ptolemy VI Philopator added a *second courtyard* while the Roman emperors built an impressive undecorated sandstone *pylon* around the portal - still well preserved – and completed the decoration of the cella and may have enlarged it. Finally, a chapel was added on the left at the time of Augustus. Only a few fragments remain of the granite *tabernacle* that was placed in the cella, though it was similar to the Ptolemaic or Roman one in the temple of Dabod now in Madrid. Beside the sanctuary, on the west bank of the Nile and in front of the Egyptian fortress of Quban, during the Ptolemaic period a city the Greeks founded a city called *Pselchis* and it became an important military centre in Roman times. From the western bank it guarded the entrance to the Alagi wadi towards the east, where the gold mines already in use during the Middle Kingdom were located.

Below, the impressive pylon of the temple of Dakkah, and, page 102, a detail of the interesting relief decorations on the sanctuary.

Opposite page, a detail
of the right corner
of the temple dedicated
to Thot with its elegantly
sculpted decorations.

On pages 104-105: the
goddess Anuqet on the inner
portal of the temple; the
cella with the stone naos;
the courtyard in front of the
temple and a detail of the
inner portal: the architrave
with the inscriptions of
cartouches of king Ptolemy
VI and his wife — and sister
— Arsinoe III.

Maharraqah

The southern boundary of Roman Nubia passed through Maharraqah dividing it from the kingdom of Meroe where there was a large market for trade between Nubian and Egyptian goods. Now known as the temple of *Ophedunia* a Roman **temple** dedicated to both Isis and Serapis, the patron of travellers, was located in Maharraqah. The cult of Serapis had been brought to Egypt by Ptolemy I who wanted to create a dynastic divinity for political purposes, that is to unite Greeks and Egyptians with a common religion.

Built about 10 km. further south of the present site and heavily restored in 1905, the building now stands about 500 metres to the east of the temple of Dakkah and has an almost square plan of 12 metres by 15, with an entrance that opens to the east and an attractive internal colonnade, though the capitals of the columns were never completed. This Roman structure with its rather particular shape has a spiral staircase that leads to the roof terrace. Inscriptions indicate that the temple was built before 37 AD and was subsequently turned into a church.

Some shots of the temple of Maharraqah with its Roman façade, and the interior with capitals and columns.

One of the most unusual features of the Maharraqah temple is, without doubt, the spiral staircase, the only one of its kind found in the temples of Nubia. In ancient times it provided access to the terrace and, still intact today, provides evidence of the great architectural expertise of the builders.

Wadi al-Sabu

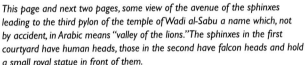

The **rock temple** dedicated to Amun-Ra and Ra Harakhte by Ramses II is situated about 120 km. from Aswan on the east bank of the Nile at Wadi al-Sabu, meaning the "Valley of the Lions", and named after the lion sphinxes. The sanctuary is now 2 km. north west of the original site and although the temple was cleaned and restored in 1905, the entire area was subsequently covered in sand. The temple is entered through a monumental doorway on both sides of which are a sphinx and a colossal statue. Through the doorway is a *first courtyard* with a short *dromos* or avenue flanked by two rows of three sphinxes. At the end was the *first pylon*, now destroyed, made of rough bricks with a stone portal, that lead to a *second courtyard* with four sphinxes (two on each side) with a lion's body and head of a falcon and a stairway to a terrace where a *second sandstone*

pylon stands 24.5 metres wide and 20 high. Only one of the four statues representing the king that stood in front of the pylon now remains. The small figure beside the leg of Ramses II is of the "royal daughter" and "royal bride" of Bent-Anat. From the pylon we reach the *third courtyard* where another stairway leads to a second terrace and to the wall of the temple cut into the mountain side.

Double doors lead to a square room with a ceiling 6 metres high. A vestibule is reached from the entrance, followed by five chapels with a cruciform arrangement, where the *central chapel* forms the inner sanctum. The temple became a Christian church in the 6th century AD and there is still some evidence of this transformation as the Egyptian reliefs were covered with plaster and on the far wall is the image of St Peter with the key of paradise in his hand.

This page and next two pages, some view of the avenue of the sphinxes leading to the third pylon of the temple of Wadi al-Sabu a name which, not by accident, in Arabic means "valley of the lions." The sphinxes in the first courtyard have human heads, those in the second have falcon heads and hold a small royal statue in front of them.

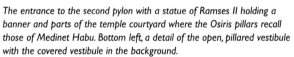

The entrance to the second pylon with a statue of Ramses II holding a banner and parts of the temple courtyard where the Osiris pillars recall those of Medinet Habu. Bottom left, a detail of the open, pillared vestibule with the covered vestibule in the background.

The bas-reliefs inside the temple of Wadi al-Sabu are in very poor condition today because they were plastered over during the Christian era. Top right, Ramses II making an offering Ra-Harakhti in a monochrome decoration in shades of yellow; right, on the east wall of the vestibule Ramses II honouring Ptah, an unidentified god and Hathor; bottom still on the east wall of the vestibule Shu, Tefnet and Nekhbet with the pharaoh, and bottom right, the sanctuary where originally Ramses II was portrayed making offerings to the gods but now all that remains is an image of Saint Peter.

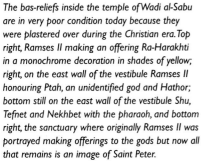

Amadah

Lying on the west bank of the river, the area of Amadah was already colonized by the Egyptians during the Middle Kingdom. Here, king Tuthmosis III dedicated a temple, later completed by his son Amenhotep II and enlarged by his grandson Tuthmosis IV, to the gods Amun-Ra and Ra Harakhte. The images of the god Amun were erased by order of Akhenaton who favoured the cult of the solar disc Aton, but were restored by Seti I. The **sanctuary** itself is quite small and well-preserved (23 metres by 10) and originally stood about 2.6 km. south of the present site. The temple was slowly moved in a single block 2600 metres over a gradient of 65 metres winching it along a device with three tracks of rollers. France provided the work force and capital for the operation and the small pronaos was dismantled and reconstructed by the Egyptian Antiquities Service. The original complex of Tuthmosis III had a *courtyard* with a portico in front, four fluted columns, a *vestibule* and three *shrines*, the most important of which is located at the back in two chapels. Tuthmosis IV made the courtyard into an atrium or *hypostyle hall* and Seti I restored the temple and built a kiosk nearby which no longer exists. The *solar boat* is in the central chapel or *cell* and carries Amun-Ra, Ra-Harakhte and king Amenhotep II who offers them jugs of wine. On the rear wall the twenty horizontal lines of the great *stele* of Amenhotep II describe the work that the pharaoh carried out in the temple during the third year of his reign and a rapid military campaign in Syria to repress a revolt.

The exterior of the temple of Amadah, begun by Tuthmosis III,
and the hypostyle room with columns and pillars in the temple of Tuthmosis IV.

Opposite page, relief carvings on the temple entrances: the royal son of Kush, the viceroy Messuy kneeling in adoration and below the viceroy Piay, also kneeling renders homage to the cartouche of king Merneptah Siptah (19th dynasty). On his back Piay wears the insignia of his rank, a short-handled flail and an ostrich feather.

On this page, top, in the sanctuary the great stele of Amenhotep II in the third year of his reign tells of a quick military campaign in Syria to put down a revolt; right, from the top, pharaoh Tuthmosis III measuring the temple with the goddess Sefekhet-Abul, "she who gives the two horns"; Amenhotep II offering bowls of milk to Amon-Ra; on the back wall of the sanctuary the solar boat with the gods Amon-Ra and Ra-Harakhti with the pharaoh.

Derr

Now entirely vanished, Derr, or El-Derr, was a large town in Nubia, once the seat of an autonomous governorate. The **rock temple** built by Ramses II and dedicated to Ra-Harakhte is carved 33 metres into the rock and has been called the "miniature Abu Simbel". It was situated on the eastern bank 11 kilometres south of its present site, which is now on the opposite bank, about 500 metres south of the temple of Amadah. The temple consists of an entrance *hall with columns* followed by a *hypostyle hall* with an unusual arrangement: three aisles are divided by six pillars and

three chapels, the central of which is the *cella*. The decorations are of military subjects: in the first room portrays battles against the Nubians, while in the second are scenes of the worship of Ra-Harakhte and of the deified Ramses II. At the back of the temple stand four statues of Ptah, Amun-Ra, the deified Ramses II and Ra-Harakhte, the same statues that are also found in the great temple at Abu Simbel. On the walls the king presents offerings to Ra-Harakhti, to Ptah and to himself "great god." The two small adjacent chapels have scenes of worship of the same gods on the walls.

*Below left, the courtyard
and vestibule of the temple.*

*The temple of Derr set into the rocks; above, the profile of
Ramses II portrayed in one of the rooms.*

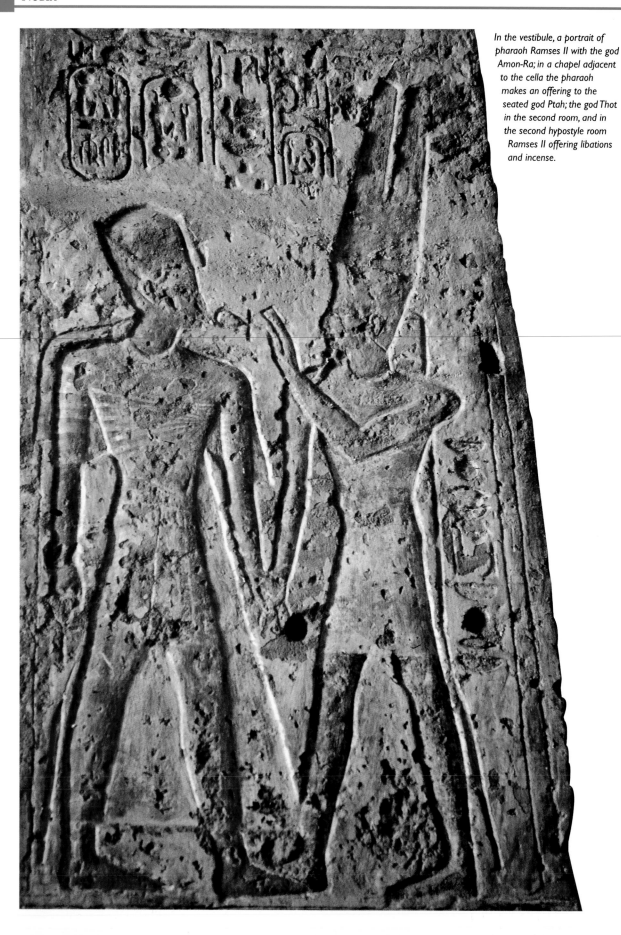

In the vestibule, a portrait of pharaoh Ramses II with the god Amon-Ra; in a chapel adjacent to the cella the pharaoh makes an offering to the seated god Ptah; the god Thot in the second room, and in the second hypostyle room Ramses II offering libations and incense.

Anibah and the Tomb of Penniut

*A*nibah (*Miam*) was an important stronghold and still remaining are part of the defensive walls, a fortress dating from the Middle Kingdom with a triple circle of walls and ramparts, the ruins of a temple, houses and storerooms from the 18th Dynasty (the reign of Tuthmosis III). The necropolis included a group of rock cut burial chambers, only one of which, created for an official of the 20th Dynasty and containing the most interesting decorations, was saved from the waters. The tomb of Penniut, whose name means "belonging to the city" was 40 kilometres from its present site and now stands a kilometre from the temple of Derr. Niut was Thebes, the greatest of cities. Penniut was the governor of Uauat during the reign of Ramses VI, about 1100 BC. After defeating Nubia the Egyptian kings of the 18th Dynasty divided the region into two provinces – Uauat in the north and Kush in the south. The area between Korosko and Abu Simbel offered good living conditions and many Egyptians lived there peacefully with the native Nubians The capital of the Egyptians, *Miam*, developed on the west bank in the area of Anibah, and had many important buildings including a temple dedicated to Horus, houses and warehouses. It was already entirely in ruins before the waters of Lake Nasser flooded the area.

Cut into the mountainside, the **tomb of Penniut**, is cruciform with an *atrium* and the *alcove for worship*,

Above, the central niche for worship with the barely roughed out statue; below, the exterior of the tomb of Penniut cut into the rock.

a form frequently used during the New Kingdom. The walls of the atrium are decorated with scenes from the life of Penniut in this world and in the next, and of his funeral. On the south wall of the atrium, to the right of the entrance, engraved on the rock, is most of a text concerning the gift of a statue, or perhaps two, of king Ramses VII

that Penniut made to the temple of Derr. He also donated some properties located near Anibah to the priests of the sanctuary as an endowment for the cult of the statue of the king. As thanks for the gift, Ramses VI sent Penniut two silver vases. The burial shaft opened from the floor of the atrium and sculpted into the rock of the alcove are three unfinished statues of divinities.

Of the many decorations on the tomb of Penniut, those on the north wall are outstanding and portray Penniut with his wife, Takha and other relatives worshipping Osiris. Unfortunately these reliefs are in very poor condition.

Qasr Ibrahim

Among the surviving ruins of what was once ancient Nubia, the only one that can boast of still standing on its original site and continuing to bear witness to its original purpose of controlling the caravans coming up the Nile Valley with goods from Africa is, without a doubt, Qasr Ibrahim. At the top of the hill from where it still dominates the Nile, this ancient *fortified settlement* may have been built during the 12th dynasty even if the oldest remains that we admire today date from a much later period, around 1000 B.C. During the pharaonic period, and for a long time afterwards, Qasr Ibrahim was also an important place of worship, linked in particular to the goddess Hathor and local expressions of Horus. The extraordinary strategic value of the site has remained through the centuries, and guaranteed its extraordinary vitality up to the beginning of the twentieth century. This is evident from walls of the fortress which was still functioning at the start of the 19th century, along with the rather ruined bas-reliefs and the broken columns of a *Christian church* that had later been converted into a mosque.

The settlement of Qasr, lapped by the waters of the lake.
Above the Nubian Christian church that had been transformed into
a mosque and is now in ruins; below the fortress of the Blemmis and
then of the Nobatis that was will active and functioning until 1812.

Gerf Hussein

The many temples Ramses II built include Gerf Hussein; it was the final stage in the pharaoh's ambitious political-religious program. This temple, dedicated to Ptah (so it was no coincidence that it was also known as the "House of Ptah"), is structurally similar to the temples of Abu Simbel and Wadi-es-Sebua, with majestic Osiris pillars, an *hypostyle* where eight niche chapels contained statues of the gods and at the back, a *sanctuary* that housed the four statues worshipped here: Ptah, Ptah Tatenen and Hathor, flanked by one of Ramses II portrayed as Ptah, with the headdress typical of the god.

Originally, an avenue of sphinxes led up to the temple. Unfortunately, this temple, too, was a victim of the construction of the Aswan dam and the creation of Lake Nasser. As opposed to the other Nubian temples, the temple of Gerf Hussein, due to the brittleness of the rock from which it was partly cut and partly built was long considered irremediably lost, definitively submerged except for the inscriptions that had been copied and the statues which had taken to safety. In truth, however, many significant parts of the temple had been saved from destruction and carefully conserved. Thus, in 2002 it was possible to proceed with a partial reconstruction (of the parts that had been built outside of the rocky wall, rather than those that had been cut into it) on the site of what is known as the "New Kalabsha": an authentic outdoor museum where the mighty pillars of the ancient "House of Ptah" once again stand in all their majesty.

The great temple of Gerf Hussein now, after a recent, partial reconstruction.

Sailing on the Nile

If it is true that Nile has always flowed through Egypt on its path from the source to the vast delta and has affected the country's life and history, it is also true that the immense river offers the most picturesque means for discovering the secrets of this extraordinary country. Seen from the craft that slowly glide along the waters of the Nile Egypt becomes even more fascinating.

With respect to the more popular tourist destinations, a cruise to discover Nubia while sailing on the calm waters of Lake Nasser is a less "classic" if not unusual, and definitely unforgettable experience. The lake was formed by the Aswan dam, an insurmountable barrier for the waters of the Nile. It is here that we can admire what archaeologists call the "collection of the dam" in all its splendour: the magnificent temples saved from the encroaching waters and rebuilt not far from their original sites. This is a truly unusual way to discover the historical region at the southern boundary of Ancient Egypt, with the incomparable

Cruises on the calm waters of the Nile and Lake Nasser are a wonderful way to discover this extraordinary region of Egypt from a most unique and fascinating vantage point.

*Lake cruisers, rocky cliffs and the remains of a glorious past:
the magnificent, famous images of the Lake Nasser region.*

"support" of comfortable vessels that smoothly ply the river. Elegant, with modern technological equipment, spacious well-fitted cabins with large picture windows, and a deck that is an excellent solarium, swimming pool, reading room and of course, bar and restaurant that offers exquisite local and international cuisine, these big ships make it possible to soak in the enchanting atmosphere of these beautiful places, lazily watching the river become a lake, letting oneself be embraced by the soft, gilded sunsets, breathing in the fragrance of history against a backdrop of majestic monuments that have even survived progress.